TALIESSIN THROUGH LOGRES

&

THE REGION OF THE SUMMER STARS

BY CHARLES WILLIAMS

With a new introduction
by Sørina Higgins

APOCRYPHILE
PRESS

THE APOCRYPHILE PRESS
1700 Shattuck Ave. #81
Berkeley, CA 94709
www.apocryphile.org

Taliessin Through Logres, by Charles Williams; first published 1938 by Oxford University Press, London, New York, and Toronto; second impression 1948; third impression 1954.

The Region of the Summer Stars, by Charles Williams; first published by Editions Poetry London, 1944; reset by Oxford University Press, 1950; reprinted 1952 and 1960.

An Introduction to Taliessin through Logres
Copyright © 2016 Sørina Higgins

ISBN 978-1-944769-31-4

Printed in the United States of America.

An Introduction to
Taliessin Through Logres

In 1938, Oxford University Press published *Taliessin Through Logres*, the first of Charles Williams' two volumes of Arthurian poetry. It is an important work of British modernism that adapts earlier traditions about Arthur (such as those by Malory and Tennyson) and is also in dialogue with Williams' contemporaries: T. S. Eliot, Ezra Pound, James Joyce, and W. B. Yeats. The poetry is technically virtuosic, musically beautiful, and conceptually complex. Like many other volumes of verse published in Britain the first half of the twentieth century, *Taliessin through Logres* is designed to reward multiple readings. It is densely packed with layers of symbolism and rich imagery that are not initially easy to understand, but that scintillate with ever greater brilliance upon repeated readings. The goal of this introduction, then, is to guide new readers through first, second, and subsequent readings of this beautiful book, aiding eager minds in appreciating its peculiar glories.

The best way to approach *Taliessin through Logres* is to read it once straight through from beginning to end, in order, as Williams designed it, taking in the main characters and plot elements without attempting to grasp the details. It is not necessary to articulate the content of the poem intellectually on a first reading or even to understand the story fully the first time through. You probably will not, because the *plot* is not the point of this collection, and, indeed, plot is often subordinated to symbolism or sound.

You may be aware that C. S. Lewis, a close friend and colleague of Charles Williams, published a commentary on these poems in 1948. This discussion, entitled "Williams and the Arthuriad," is extraordinarily helpful. Lewis gives useful insights into many aspects of Williams' poetry, and I highly recommend it as a companion to his poems. However, one point that Lewis makes is, I believe, wrong. In his discussion, he recommends that readers interweave the twenty-four poems of *Taliessin through Logres* with the eight longer pieces from *The Region of the Summer Stars* (published in 1944). Lewis suggests a reading order that arranges the poems chronologically according to a simple reading of events they contain. However, doing this misses the poetic, narrative, logical, and spiritual structure of *Taliessin through Logres.*[1] This book has its own internal unity, which can only be experienced by reading the poems in the order in which Williams arranged them. This is the best and most immersive way to encounter them.[2]

On a second reading, you can slow down and take time to appreciate the musical aspects of the verses. Read purely for the sounds and the images Williams creates in this sensuous poetry. Revel in the phonoaesthetics and the lavish visual descriptions. This is beautiful writing, rich with musical appeal and dancing with gorgeous imagery. I recommend a purely aesthetic immersion, in which you listen as if you are attending a chamber concert of string instruments and look as if you are walking through galleries of abstract oil paintings. Luxuriate in luscious sentences like this one from "The Vision of the Empire":

> The organic body sang together;
> dialects of the world sprang in Byzantium;
> back they rang to sing in Byzantium;
> the streets repeat the sound of the Throne. (lines 1–4)

Delight in the imagery and syntax of this series of questions from a lover to his beloved in "Bors to Elayne: On the Fish of Broceliande":

> A forest of the creatures: was it of you? no?
> monstrous beasts in the trees, birds flying the flood,
> and I plucked a fish from a stream that flowed to the sea:
> from you? for you? shall I drop the fish in your hand?
> in your hand's pool? a bright-scaled, red-tailed fish
> to dart and drive up the channel of your arm? (lines 10–15).

---

1   Curiously, there is an analogous situation with C. S. Lewis' Narnia chronicles; readers and publishers debate about whether to read them in the order in which he first published them or in an artificial re-arrangement that is somewhat chronological. Any thoughtful examination of the themes of the Narnia books, however, leads to the obvious conclusion that they are best read in the original, published order. Starting with *The Lion, the Witch and the Wardrobe* leads a reader through Narnian history, a progressive revelation of Aslan's character, an experience of unfolding salvation and eschatology, and the deep themes of Christological providence in the most effective manner. The same is true for *Taliessin through Logres* and *The Region of the Summer Stars*: starting with a sense of mystery about Taliessin's origins and his place in Arthur's kingdom leads a reader into the unfurling fascination with the Matter of Britain.

2   Incidentally, Williams intended to rewrite all of his Arthurian poems into a longer narrative cycle, in which he himself would have rewoven the previously-published pieces into a whole mythical fabric, but he never did so. Without that completed work, it is vain to speculate on a useful artificial order. It is better to take the poems as he presented them on a first reading.

Introduction

When you get to the masterful, one-sentence, thirty-six-line lyric "Taliesin's Song of the Unicorn," read it in one long breath, not pausing to parse the grammar. Let the rhythm of each poem carry you at its own pace.

It is in the area of technique that Williams sits most comfortably in the company of his fellow Modernists. In his mature works, he broke free from stilted, traditional meters and clanging, predictable end-rhymes. This was largely due to his editing of an edition of Gerard Manley Hopkins' poems in 1932; after this time, Williams' poetry became more and more challenging and beautiful.

Alliteration is one of his primary devices. He is not writing quasi-Anglo Saxon alliterative verse, as his friend J. R. R. Tolkien did, but rather deploying skillfully-placed alliterations for sonic appeal. "Taliesin's Song of the Unicorn" begins:

> Shouldering shapes of the skies of Broceliande
> are rumours in the flesh of Caucasia; they raid the west,
> clattering with shining hooves, in myth scanned—(lines 1–3)

Notice the multiple, varied "s" sounds in the first line: sh-, sk-, ce- (and also perhaps the "z" sound at the end of "skies"). They provide a pleasant balance of aural similarity and difference. This careful arrangement of "s" sounds continues in the next two lines, but there they are largely in unaccented syllables so that the repetition does not become tedious. Keep an ear open for the subtle effects of alliteration throughout the poems.

The choice of *which* sound to choose for alliteration is also adroit. Writers and scholars have developed theories about the psychological effects of certain phonemes[3]: low-pitched vowels, such as "oh" and "oo," for example, are cool and soothing and smooth, but can also evoke gloom, doom, and the tomb. This line, from the "Prelude," uses deep vowel sounds powerfully: "The blind rulers of Logres" (line 10). Their doom is inherent in the dark colors painted in that line. High-pitched vowels, such as "ee," feel like a shriek or a screech or a scream, but could also be cheery or sweet. Two lines later, the "Prelude" says: "The seals of the saints were broken; the chairs of the Table reeled" (line 12). You can hear the feet of the chairs

---

3   Refer to the book *Western Wind* by Frederick Nims and David Mason for more on this auditory theory.

scraping across the stone floor of Camelot as the knights leap up and leave the fellowship of the Round Table.

Hard consonants, such as k, t, and p, sound sharp, abrupt, and even violent. Sustained consonants, such as l, m, and n, are liquid and mellifluous. Listen to how these combinations of vowels and consonants work together in this description of dancing girls:

> The bright blades shone in the craft of the dancing war;
> the stripped maids laugh for joy of the province,
> bearing in themselves the shape of the province
> founded in the base of space,
> in the rounded bottom of the Emperor's glory.
>
> ("The Vision of the Empire" lines 35–39)

The poem rejoices in the settled, natural pleasure of the women's bodies and in the ordered patterns and rhythms of God's universe.

Rhyme is also used carefully throughout *Taliessin through Logres*, rarely at the ends of lines, but embedded wherever it can have greatest effect. Here is an instance of combined end- and internal rhyme, for a powerful effect that matches the violence depicted:

> who of the pirates saw? none stopped;
> they cropped and lopped Logres; they struck deep,
> and their luck held; only support lacked.
>
> ("Mount Badon" lines 11–13)

Notice also the hard consonants that emphasize the hacking of the swords in the battle.

Yet it is in the areas of rhythm and syntax that Williams excels most highly. He employs a great variety of metrical devices throughout this volume, balancing the line against the sentence and both against the meter. "Taliessin's Song of the Unicorn," again, is an ideal showcase of his skill. Here again are the opening lines of that thirty-six-line, one-sentence lyric:

> Shouldering shapes of the skies of Broceliande
> are rumours in the flesh of Caucasia; they raid the west,
> clattering with shining hooves, in myth scanned—
> centaur, gryphon, but lordlier for verse is the crest
> of the unicorn, the quick panting unicorn; he will come...

Each of those lines has five strong stresses. And yet nothing could be further from the pedestrian iambs of a minor poet. Line one has twelve syllables; line two has fourteen; line three has ten, but they are very unequally stressed; line four has thirteen; and line five has a magisterial fifteen. These packed lines read not unlike Hopkins' sprung rhythm, in which many unstressed, alliterated or assonant or otherwise consonant syllables are crowded into a line that still maintains a small number of stresses. The result is rich, energetic, vivid verse, full of visual and physical descriptions, that has a visceral impact on a reader. The syntax is difficult, with frequently-delayed verbs or inverted subjects. The whole poem proceeds as a series of interlocked clauses, an imagistic chain that slides, link by link, through the reader's imagination. There is an archetypal story in this poem, but it is inseparable from the way in which the piece is constructed, as all the elements together created its "meaning"—about the power of the poet and the magical art of the poet.

Those, then, are some of the beauties you may desire to enjoy on a second reading. When you return for a third reading, you will be ready to follow the story. You still will not need to mentally annotate every symbol, occult reference, or idiomatic phrase; it will be enough, at this stage, to understand the people, places, events of the poems. The main locations are as follows.

Logres is Arthur's kingdom on the island of Britain. In Williams' mythology, it is represented as the head or brain of the Empire. There, Arthur establishes his kingdom at Camelot along the Thames river. Carbonek is the castle of King Pelles, a wounded king who guards the Holy Grail. Broceliande is a mysterious forest in the West, where people go mad if they wander too long. Further West, somewhere over the sea, lies the holy island of Sarras, the land of the Trinity. In Williams' myth, England is a province of a Romano-Byzantine Empire, its capital at Constantinople, which represents the Kingdom of God on earth.

Here is a synopsis of the action as it unfolds in *Taliessin through Logres*, poem by poem. You may find it useful to read this entire synopsis first, or to bookmark it and return to read each section as you work your way through the corresponding poems.

The "Prelude" lays out the political and spiritual situation in which Williams' Arthurian mythology takes place. His Arthur is one actor on a vast European stage, rather than a localized Romano-British monarch. His Logres is a province of a vast Empire, and the actions of public and private persons at home in England have international consequences. The historical details are somewhat fictionalized: Williams compresses one thousand years of European history down into the span of Arthur's lifetime, beginning with the Battle of Badon Hill around the year 500 A.D. and ending with the fall of Constantinople to the Ottoman Turks in 1453. He conflates the Roman and Byzantine empires, creating an imaginary theological-political Kingdom of God on earth. He also erases the East-West schism of the Church for his own theological purposes, focusing on Christian unity. He emphasizes that this is a time period when news of the Christian Gospel is racing across Europe, transforming the globe, until Britain's sins at home and the advance of Islam abroad interfere with the realization of the doctrine of Incarnation. It is unclear who is the narrator of this first poem; it may be Taliessin, who is the first character you will meet.

Taliessin is a poet, harp-player, and singer. There was a real, historical Celtic poet named Taliesin[4] in the sixth century, and some of his poetry is extant (as well as a great deal of poetry attributed to him that is likely to have been written much later). When he appears to narrate "Taliessin's Return to Logres" in the first person, however, he is an enigma. All that he says about himself is that he is returning to "Logres" (which is a traditional name for Arthur's righteous realm). As the poem progresses, it becomes clear that Taliessin unites two identities in himself: he is a Druid, with pagan power and poetry; he is also a Christian who has been traveling on the Roman road and calls upon God under the title "the Mercy." He unites pagan magic and Christian mysticism in himself. He brings these united contraries with him into Arthur's camp. Therefore, he sets up the spiritual and poetic themes that will be important in Williams' version of Arthur's kingdom.

Then Taliessin shares "The Vision of the Empire," which reveals that he has travelled across Europe to Byzantium: to the capital city, Constantinople.

---

4   Tennyson changed the spelling of the poet's name to 'Taliessin' in his own Arthurian cycle. Grevel Lindop writes that Williams followed this spelling, "perhaps to clarify the pronunciation: four syllables, with the stress on the third: 'Tally-ESS-in'" (*The Third Inkling* 227).

There, he heard the Gospel. He also had a holistic spiritual vision of the whole Empire working together, like one great body, under the Emperor's command. He is communicating this prophetic insight to Arthur, because it will be the inspiration and motivation for Arthur's heavenly kingdom-on-earth, Logres.

This image of the empire as a body is one of Williams' most innovative and essential ideas. He worked with an artist at Oxford University Press, Lynton Lamb, to draw a "gynocomorphical" map: a drawing of a nude woman superimposed over an image of Europe. Taliessin pictures the Empire as a female body, and he often refers to provinces (or "themes") of the Empire by their anatomical correspondences. This imagery need not be a hindrance, however; merely think of the metaphor of the Church as the body of Christ, and you will grasp the general idea.

While Taliessin is sharing his vison of the Empire, Williams also retells his Myth of the Fall of Man. The best preparation for understanding his view of the Original Sin is found in *He Came Down from Heaven*, Williams' most highly idiosyncratic theological work. Chapter II of *He Came Down*, "The Myth of the Alteration in Knowledge," presents a new reading of Genesis chapter three. Williams suggests that only God can know evil without being touched by it or participating in it. The first humans desired the Knowledge of Good and Evil—but there was no way for them to know evil without being implicated in it. Against God's command, they insisted on knowing evil. God, having granted them free will, consented. He let them know Evil. But they could not simply know *about* it; they could only know it in an experiential sense. In French, they couldn't know Evil in the sense of *savoir*; they must know it in the sense of *connaître*. As a result, they got to know evil from the inside out: they experienced death, suffering, and cruelty—but they also knew Good as if it were evil. Their relationship with the Good was also tainted. The first sin, then, was a sin of knowledge, not of desire, or pride, or any of the other vices that are often considered the Original Sin. The poem "The Vision of the Empire" is another retelling of this same myth of the fall, focusing on corrupted knowledge as the Original Sin.

Taliessin tells Arthur all about the Emperor's vision for his kingdom, and then in "The Calling of Arthur," Merlin meets Arthur on the road and orders him to build Camelot. The last of the corrupt kings in London dies, and Arthur begins his work. Lancelot comes to join him. Order begins to take shape and to set up its patterns in Logres. Again, the narrative perspective is unclear in this poem, but it may again be by Taliessin in his role as court poet, perhaps as a kind of chronicler recording the events of Arthur's calling and kingship.

Next, Arthur must fight the Battle of "Mount Badon" to beat back the invading Saxon "pirates" (as Williams calls them). All his best knights are there, commanding divisions of his army: Lancelot, Gawaine, and Bors. Taliessin has not only been appointed King's poet; he is also the King's Captain of the Horse, commanding the mounted division. He does not narrate this poem; it is told in the third person by some unknown watcher with an omniscient perspective. Taliessin watches the battle, waiting for the precise moment to strike. At the same time, he envisions Virgil writing the Aeneid, waiting for just the right word to finish a line. Virgil finds the word, Taliessin sees the enemy's weak point, and the cavalry charges. The battle is won; Logres is established, and Arthur's kingship assured.

"The Crowning of Arthur" follows the battle, in a heraldic poem filled with the blazing colors and beasts of the knights' and ladies' coats-of-arms. This is another omniscient third-person piece. Merlin watches all the animals on the banners swirling in Camelot, and he senses things to come. Arthur asks himself the vital question: Do I exist to serve the kingdom, or does the kingdom exist to serve me? Merlin then sees the Dolorous Blow: the wicked spear-thrust by which Balan wounded King Pelles, sealing Camelot's doom. This suggests that Arthur answered his question wrongly, setting himself above the kingdom and refusing to serve.

Arthur's selfishness is the first example of the theme of this whole book: *Love Gone Wrong.* There are many kinds of love in these poems, and most of them are perverted, twisted, and doomed.

But before Logres goes wrong, Taliessin, the court poet, sings his debut: "Taliessin's Song of the Unicorn." We are to assume that these are actually the lyrics of a song Taliessin performed for the court at Camelot soon after its establishment. It is a virtuosic performance: a masterpiece of modernist verse. Its one long sentence unwinds with speed and grace, weaving Williams' major themes into one contained metaphor. It is sexual, passionate, shocking, and powerful. The poem draws a receptive reader into a strange, dangerous, mysterious world where a maiden might submit to being impaled by a mythical beast, leaving both the woman and the reader wounded and moved.

Arthur's knights, too, were touched when they heard this song sung in court. The first to speak of his wounding is Sir Bors—the only example in the poetry of Love Gone Right. In "Bors to Elayne: The Fish of Broceliande," he rides home from court to visit his wife, sings or speaks this poem to her, and gives her a "fish" that he has "plucked" out of Taliessin's song, and it swims up her veins and through her body, which he worships. The fish is love, certainly, but it is also myth, truth, and meaning. The fish is an emblem of Williams' distinctive Romantic Theology: embodied, personified, brought to life as an animal, and in Elayne's body. It is the Affirmative Way in action.

Following Arthur's military victory, the establishment of his kingdom, and the display of domestic love in action at the heart of the kingdom, "Taliessin in the School of the Poets" gives a lesson on the composition of verse. In the third person, Taliessin visits and lectures the young writers on order, anatomy, law, and empire. So a performance-piece by Taliessin is embedded into this poem about Taliessin.

While still at the school of the poets, Taliessin recites a poem for them, presumably as an example of great verse: "Taliessin on the Death of Virgil." Like the one about the unicorn, we are to read this poem as an example of Taliessin's poems written at Camelot, integrated into the cycle. As Bors' love song to Elayne was an expression of Romantic Theology, so this poem brings to life The Way of Exchange. In it, Taliessin tells how Virgil died and was falling, falling, falling, on his way to the grave, on his way to hell. But later readers, who would be saved by reading Virgil's works, reached back from the future and gave him eternal salvation: "Virgil was fathered of his friends. / He lived in their ends. / He was set on the marble of exchange." Thus Williams lays the theological foundation for Logres in simultaneity, service, poetry, romantic theology, and exchange.

Immediately after this glorious beginning, we see one of the Loves Gone Wrong in "The Coming of Palomides." This is a remarkable poem, as it introduces a whole new perspective. A Muslim warrior travels from Iran to become a Knight of the Round Table. On the way, he lands in Cornwall, where he is offered hospitality by King Mark—and sets eyes upon Iseult. Tristam is there, too, and all three men are in love with Iseult in one way or another. King Mark is oblivious to his rivals; Iseult has eyes only for

Tristram; and Palomides sings her a love song about her arm's perfect geometry. He sings this poem in the first person, giving his own perception of his unrequited love. He catches a glimpse of her true, perfected nature and sees the meaning of the universe. But then she moves, she speaks, and her imperfections are revealed. His vision flees away. He determines to chase it, this "questing beast," this "division stretched between / the queen's identity and the queen," and make something of himself before he will submit to conversion and baptism.

"Lamorack and the Queen Morgause of Orkney" is the tale of another Love Gone Wrong, and another poem told by the jaded lover from his own perspective. Lamorack, Knight of the Table, brother of Sir Percivale, travels north and sees the stone sculptures carved on the coasts of the Orkney Islands. He also sees Queen Morgause, the living image of her cold stone ancestors, and his heart is bruised and broken on her hardness. Back in Camelot, Lamorack talks to Merlin, who sees a vision of Morgause and her brother Arthur committing incest. From their evil union a child will be born, "the web of all our doom," Mordred.

But that doom is still in the future. Arthur, secure, begins minting coins. Sir Bors—the image of Love Gone Right—reports to his wife the conversations the economic committee had about the minting of coins in the poem "Bors to Elayne: on the King's Coins." Taliessin, Bors says, is afraid of the coins: they are symbols, set loose from verse, running unchecked about the kingdom, separating exchange from community. But Sir Kay and the Archbishop think the coins are an excellent idea, because "money is a medium of exchange."

The encounter in "The Star of Percivale" is a much more ambiguous love, told by an unidentified narrator. A slave girl hears Taliessin singing and conceives a passion for him. He tells her to love someone else instead—presumably Christ—but the reader is left unsure whether she is able to make that great leap. Meanwhile, others commit idolatry: while celebrating the Eucharist, Balan is thrust through with anger, Arthur sees only himself in the bread and wine, and Lancelot sees only Guinevere upon the altar.

Next, Taliessin comes across a slave girl—possibly the same one who heard him singing—who has been set in the stocks. He speaks to her, and her pride breaks, and she is set free. Her untied hands make "The Ascent of the Spear," which is a symbol of her spiritual uplifting. This follows thematically on the concepts of order, discipline, and hierarchy that have been set up through the cycle so far.

And then it is Taliessin's turn to fall in love. He is lying on a wall on a stormy July afternoon, watching a slave draw water, and writing a poem in which is uses the scars on the slave's back as a metaphor. He looks up and sees "The Sister of Percivale." Her name is Blanchefleur (later Dindrane), and she will be the focus of his Romantic Theology. But he does not narrate this poem—it is our ambiguous third-person narrator again—and the story of their love does not occur in this poetic cycle; it was published six years later in *The Region of the Summer Stars*.

The next Love Gone Wrong is the story of Lancelot and Guinevere—or, rather, the story of Lancelot, Helayne, and "The Son of Lancelot." You may know the tale, but Williams adds startling twists, through his omniscient perspective. Lancelot comes to Carbonek, the castle of the Hallows, where King Pelles lives, and is beguiled by magic into thinking Helayne was Guinevere. Doubly unfaithful to his knightly vows to Arthur and his chivalric vows to Guinevere as her courtly lover, he sleeps with Helayne. Their child will be Galahad, the pure knight, the High Prince, the achiever of the Grail. But in Williams' poem, these events are not directly related in the narrative. Instead, Merlin, high in a tower, watches all things by his magic. Merlin sees winter and famine gripping the kingdom. He sees the Grail quest and the Islamic invasions. And then… he sees Lancelot waking, realizing what he has done—and running mad, *turning into a wolf*, living in a nine-month nightmare, "a delirium of lycanthropy." Lancelot, crazy, hungry, desires nothing for those nine months but to devour his own son. Merlin sees this and leaves the vision, leaping into action in real time. Merlin turns himself into a great, white wolf, and lopes across the kingdom to meet Lancelot—a great, grey, lean, shaggy wolf—and they arrive at Carbonek just as the child is born. The wolves leap and clash. At the same moment, the Emperor in Byzantium sends out his army against heretics. The Merlin-wolf sends the Lancelot-wolf crashing to the ground. Merlin's sister, Brisen, takes the baby from his mother and ties him on Merlin's furry back. Merlin gallops away and brings the baby safely to Blanchefleur, who is a nun at Almesbury. There, she will serve as Galahad's foster-mother.

Lancelot loses the wolf-shape and is tended in Carbonek. By Easter, he is well and can ride for Camelot.

Meanwhile, Palomides gets to speak for himself again in the stark poem "Palomides Before his Christening." The Saracen tries to catch the Questing Beast. It leads him to a stony cave, where he lies, lonely, skeletal, longing for bones to lie down beside his bones for company. Brought to nothing, he is humbled and decides to submit to baptism.

And then the cycle draws near its climax in "The Coming of Galahad." The High Prince, now a young man, arrives at Camelot. The time in between his birth and his coming is telescoped into that one poem of Palomides' lean years. When Galahad comes, there is great rejoicing in the hall. He is set by ritual substitution in King Arthur's bed, as if he is the child of Arthur and Guinevere instead of the son of Lancelot and Helayne. He is the vicarious prince of the realm. A child of sin, he will be the means of grace. At his coming, the Grail is manifested in Camelot.

But the reader does not get to watch that powerful scene of the Grail's revelation first-hand. No, it is discussed behind the scenes, as it were, by Taliessin, Gareth, and a slave-girl—out among the kitchen-waste and sewage-pits of the castle. Even the refuse, the rubbish, and the dung are parts of the grand pattern of being. And thus, after the arrival of Galahad and the revelation of the Grail, it is time for "The Departure of Merlin." He sails away, leaving all things apparently in order.

Palomides has one final chance to speak in his own voice in "The Death of Palomides." He sees his end drawing near. He is baptized, then goes to study Kabbalah, learning about the hard way of endurance God has granted him, and then ends his poem as he senses "this my dying." But he ends praising God for the hard and true path on which He led him.

The last two poems return to the omniscient narrator. In "Percivale at Carbonek," Percivale, Bors, and Galahad come to Pelles's castle to achieve the Grail. Then the cycle skips ahead again, to the end, or nearly the end, of the story. The three Grail Knights are on a ship, sailing away on "The Last Voyage." It is not clear whether they have the Grail with them, or whether they are sailing to find it. They are sailing to Sarras, the land of the Trinity. Also on the ship is the dead body of Blanchefleur. She gave her blood to save another woman's life in the ultimate act of Exchange. As they sail, Galahad sings a litany for all the kingdom's losses—and in this way the reader learns that Logres has been destroyed. Dinadan has been murdered by Agravaine. Lamorack has been killed in an ambush. The sons of Morgause have slain their mother. Gawaine has "hewed the Table in twain." Gawaine's violence is presumably vengeance for the accidental death of his brothers, but that is not recounted in Williams' version of the tale. All of this death and destruction follows the scandal of Lancelot and Guinevere's adultery, but again, Williams does not mention that, leaving it to the reader's knowledge of the tradition.

At the end of the penultimate poem, "The Last Voyage":

> In Logres the King's friend landed, Lancelot of Gaul.
> Taliessin at Canterbury met him with the news
> of Arthur's death and the overthrow of Mordred.
> ...
> Logres was withdrawn to Carbonek; it became Britain.
> (lines 120–23, 125)

And that would be the end of the story—betrayal, infidelity, defeat, death—except that this is Charles Williams' story. Death is not the end. Lancelot performs a Mass—Lancelot, who is not a priest, and who is arguably the author of much of the horror, becomes the servant and officiant at Christ's table. Taliessin attends and helps to sing some of the liturgy. During this Mass, several substitutions take place. It appears that Pelles has been healed, and somehow he and Arthur make an exchange, such that the dead King is present at the Mass. Guinevere, through another substitution, becomes Galahad's mother. Her substitution is also somehow responsible for Arthur's exchange. It might be an exaggeration to say that Lancelot's celebration of the Eucharist heals all things, but the poem ends in joy. The members of Taliessin's Company pray for the kingdom. It seems that the political realm of Logres has failed, but the spiritual kingdom of the Grail lives on in the prayers of those few who remain and in the company of all the co-inherent living and dead.

That, then, is the "plot" of *Taliessin through Logres*. If you work your way through with this summary in hand, then you can go on to a fourth and fifth and subsequent readings in which you move deeper, through the layers, tracing the anatomical imagery, searching for the working-out of Williams' major themes, learning the significance of recurrent phrases and images, and developing a key to his symbolic imagery.

The anatomical geometry is one of the most important themes to notice. Williams associates each country on the map of Europe with a part of the human body. Then he connects each of those to a sign of the zodiac and to a virtue. He learned this method of symbolic layering from the Christian, occult secret societies in which he spent perhaps twenty years of his adult life and whose truths he was committed to promulgating. The more deeply you dig into these poems, the more associations you will notice among places, spiritual qualities, and physical actions. These reveal that the poems are not only about King Arthur; they are about the journey of the soul toward God.

Another important element is the transformation of sin into grace. Many people fall into adulterous love in these poems, but for many of the characters, even these forbidden loves become a means of charity and redemption. Lancelot's liaison with Helayne—while it remains a dreadful sin against God, Arthur, and Guinevere (not to mention Helayne herself, who is abandoned and whose baby is taken from her!)—leads to the birth of Galahad, who is the Christ-figure in this story.

A notable feature of Williams' work is his characteristic syncretism. He is equally comfortable using druidic, astrological, alchemical, and Christian imagery. This is similar to his approach to history, in which he conflates events from various time periods and from legend to create his own myth. His approach is akin to Tolkien and Lewis' idea of True Myth, in which all human mythologies point to the historical reality of Christ's Incarnation and Passion, but it is more strange.

These features are a large part of what makes Williams stand out in the crowded field of twentieth-century British writers of Arthuriana. Putting Williams' Arthurian works in their historical context may be illuminating. There were many works of literature about Arthur in Great Britain in the period of the two World Wars. These include T. S. Eliot's *The Waste Land* (1922); Thomas Hardy's *Tragedy of Isolde* (1923), John Masefield's *The Midnight Folk* (1927), *Midsummer Night and Other Tales in Verse* (1928), *The Box of Delights* (1935), and many short poems; John Cowper Powys' *A Glastonbury Romance* (1932) and *Porius* (1951); David Jones' *In Parenthesis* (1937) and *The Anathemata* (1952); and T. H. White's *Once and Future King* (1938–58). During this time, Arthur was sometimes used as a powerful figure of social cohesion, moral rectitude, and military might during the terrible conflicts in which Britain was engaged, or he was employed to question war, chivalry, and victory.

Several of Williams' literary predecessors, teachers, colleagues, students, and friends also joined the Arthurian conversation: George MacDonald (1824–1905), William Morris (1834–96), A. E. Waite (1857–1942), Arthur Machen (1863–1947), G. K. Chesterton (1874–1936), Roger Lancelyn Green (1918–87), and John Heath-Stubbs (1918–2006) each wrote Arthurian works and had some influence on or connection with Williams. And, closest of all, each of the major members of "The Inklings"—the gathering of Oxford Christian writers including C. S. Lewis and J. R. R. Tolkien which Williams joined in 1939—wrote letters, poetry, fiction, or performance pieces with Arthurian elements. Their professional knowledge of medieval and Renaissance literature (especially Lewis' and Tolkien's) gave them the ability to read earlier Arthurian materials with great accuracy, detail, and interpretive depth, and apply them to their own time's need for redemption. They were also soldiers who had fought in World War One, so their insights into military glory and infamy are valuable. And they were creative professionals whose Arthuriana contain incisive critiques of their own times and visions of utopian or dystopian futures evolving out of contemporary decisions.

Williams participated vigorously in the literary culture of his own times. He was keenly aware of the disputes and dialogues of his contemporaries and eagerly contributed his own experimental poetry to the developments of Modernism. It is in this historical context—the ravages of two world wars, the advancements of science and technology, the spiritual responses of religious communities and occult secret societies, and the breakdown of iambic pentameter—that a reader can best understand *Taliessin through Logres*.

Taliessin through Logres, then, was both relevant and unique in its time. His choice of short, lyric poems using a modernist technique is one distinctive feature—most others were novels, dramas, or longer poems in archaic forms. His use of Galahad as a salvific figure sprung from sin is idiomatic, as is his approach to history and legend. Yet it is his attempt to make the spiritual significance of the Grail the absolute center and the unifying feature of the whole myth that truly sets him apart. While many other poets, Medieval to Modern, had told the Quest for the Holy Grail, none—Williams believed—had succeeded in relating every character and every event to it in ways that revealed its deep spiritual significance. Whether he achieved the Grail in this sense or not, each reader must determine. In any case, the poetry will reward repeat visits and will enrich your appreciation of Arthurian legends, twentieth-century British literature, and the mythopoeic vision of the Inklings.

— SØRINA HIGGINS

Contents

Unde est, quod non operatio propria propter
essentiam, sed haec propter illam habet ut
sit.

De Monarchia, I, iii.

Prelude

I

Recalcitrant tribes heard ;
orthodox wisdom sprang in Caucasia and Thule ;
the glory of the Emperor stretched to the ends of the world.

In the season of midmost Sophia
the word of the Emperor established a kingdom in Britain ;
they sang in Sophia the immaculate conception of wisdom.

Carbonek, Camelot, Caucasia,
were gates and containers, intermediations of light ;
geography breathing geometry, the double-fledged Logos.

II

The blind rulers of Logres
nourished the land on a fallacy of rational virtue ;
the seals of the saints were broken ; the chairs of the Table
    reeled.

Galahad quickened in the Mercy ;
but history began ; the Moslem stormed Byzantium ;
lost was the glory, lost the power and kingdom.

Call on the hills to hide us
lest, men said in the City, the lord of charity
ride in the starlight, sole flash of the Emperor's glory.

III

Evil and good were twins
once in the alleys of Ispahan ; the Moslem
crying *Alla il Alla* destroyed the dualism of Persia.

Caucasia fell to the Moslem ;
the mamelukes seized the ancient cornland of Empire.
Union is breached ; the imams stand in Sophia.

Good is God, the muezzin
calls, but lost is the light on the hills of Caucasia,
glory of the Emperor, glory of substantial being.

Taliessin's Return to Logres

The seas were left behind;
in a harbour of Logres
lightly I came to land
under a roaring wind.
Strained were the golden sails,
the masts of the galley creaked
as it rode for the Golden Horn
and I for the hills of Wales.

In a train of golden cars
the Emperor went above,
for over me in my riding
shot seven golden stars,
as if while the great oaks stood,
straining, creaking, around,
seven times the golden sickle
flashed in the Druid wood.

Covered on my back,
untouched, my harp had hung;
its notes sprang to sound
as I took the blindfold track,
the road that runs from tales,
through the darkness where Circe's son
sings to the truants of towns
in a forest of nightingales.

The beast ran in the wood
that had lost the man's mind;
on a path harder than death
spectral shapes stood
propped against trees;
they gazed as I rode by;
fast after me poured
the light of flooding seas.

But I was Druid-sprung;
I cast my heart in the way;
all the Mercy I called
to give courage to my tongue.
As I came by Broceliande
a diagram played in the night,
where either the golden sickle
flashed, or a signalling hand.

Away on the southern seas
was the creaking of the mast;
beyond the Roman road
was the creaking of the trees.
Beyond the farms and the fallows
the sickle of a golden arm
that gathered fate in the forest
in a stretched palm caught the hallows.

At the falling of the first
chaos behind me checked;
at the falling of the second
the wood showed the worst;

at the falling of the third
I had come to the king's camp ;
the harp on my back
syllabled the signal word.

I saw a Druid light
burn through the Druid hills,
as the hooves of King Arthur's horse
rounded me in the night.
I heard the running of flame
faster than fast through Logres
into the camp by the hazels
I Taliessin came.

The Vision of the Empire

α

The organic body sang together;
dialects of the world sprang in Byzantium;
back they rang to sing in Byzantium;
the streets repeat the sound of the Throne.

The Acts issue from the Throne.
Under it, translating the Greek minuscula
to minds of the tribes, the identities of creation
phenomenally abating to kinds and kindreds,
the household inscribes the Acts of the Emperor;
the logothetes run down the porphyry stair
bearing the missives through the area of empire.

Taliessin walked through the hither angels,
from the exposition of grace to the place of images.
The morn brightened on the Golden Horn;
he heard behind him the chariots' clatter
that bore a new matter to all the dialects;
he saw the nuntii loosened on the currents
over the sea, in the mechanism of motion,
rowers' arms jointed to the imperial oars.
Chariots and galleys sprang from the shores;
the messengers were borne over sea and land.
The king's poet gazed in the mirror of the Horn.

β

The morn rose on the Golden Horn.
I saw the identities imaged in a sapphire sea :
beyond Sinai Ararat, beyond Ararat Elburz—
light-sprinkling, flaked-snow-sparkling,
chastities of ranged peaks of Caucasus,
snow's glow on the world's brows
changed with deep vales of verdure.
The missives of identity came from the scribes
where the tribes gather and keep holiday
on the name-day and birthday of their father the Emperor.
The Empire's sun shone on each round mound,
double fortalices defending dales of fertility.
The bright blades shone in the craft of the dancing war ;
the stripped maids laughed for joy of the province,
bearing in themselves the shape of the province
founded in the base of space,
in the rounded bottom of the Emperor's glory.
Spines were strengthened, loves settled ;
tossed through aerial gulfs of empire
the lost name, the fool's shame,
fame and frame of lovers in lowlands of Caucasia,
rang round snowy Elburz.
The organic body sang together.

γ

Elburz rose in the Golden Horn.
South from the sea-bone, Thule, the skull-stone,
herbage of lone rock,
the scheme of Logres, the theme of the design of the Empire,

rose in balance and weight, freight of government with
    glory.
Merlin, time's metre, climbs through prisms and lines ;
over near Camelot and far Carbonek,
over the Perilous Sell, the See of union,
the phosphor of Percivale's philosophical star shines.
Lancelot's lion, bewildered by the smell of adoration,
roars round Guinevere's lordly body.
Merlin defines, in blazons of the brain,
shield upon shield, station upon station ;
and the roads resound with the galloping lords.
The swords flash ; the pirates fly ;
the Table stands rigid in the king's hall,
and over their seats the plotted arms of the soul,
which are their feats and the whole history of Logres.
Down the imperial highroad the white nuntius rides
to heighten the hearts of Lateran, Gaul, and Logres.

ϑ

The milk rises in the breasts of Gaul,
trigonometrical milk of doctrine.
Man sucks it ; his joints harden,
sucking logic, learning, law,
drawing on the breasts of *intelligo* and *credo*.
I, Taliessin, born of the Druids by the sea,
drank also in the schools of Gaul ;
I have drunk at the tables of all the doctors ;
I have modulated song to the waters of Logres,
the running of Thames, the tidal basins.
I heard the iron chariots on the roads of Gaul,

but the fleets took me, distances of the sea ;
the dialect of Logres was an aspect of Byzantium ; ·
the grand art was taught in the heart of the harbours of Arthur.

ε

The mist rolled down the edge of an old sun ;
mammoth and bear prowled on the broad ledge of the
  shoulders.
Strength articulated itself in morals
of arms, joints, wrists, hands ;
the planes of palms, the mid-points of hid cones,
opened in Lombardy, the cone's point in Rome,
seminal of knowledge, pontifex of the Arval college
of spiralling instincts, all roads (active and passive) from Rome,
to be bridge-builders in Gaul, clerks of audience in Byzantium.
Finger-nails, weaklings of seedtime, scratched the soil
till by iron nails the toil was finished in the time of our need,
the sublime circle of the cone's bottom, the seed-springing
  surrender :
hands of incantation changed to hands of adoration,
the quintuple psalm, the pointing of Lateran :
active and passive in a single mystery,
a single sudden flash of identity,
the heart-breaking manual acts of the Pope.

ζ

Why moves the Pope in the marches of the Empire?
why do the golden palaces pale to the Papal
vesture, flesh and bone of reparation ?
what was the crossing of the will of the Emperor ?

η

The Adam in the hollow of Jerusalem respired :
softly their thought twined to its end,
crying : *O parent, O forkèd friend,*
am I not too long meanly retired
in the poor space of joy's single dimension ?
Does not God vision the principles at war ?
Let us grow to the height of God and the Emperor :
Let us gaze, son of man, on the Acts in contention.

The Adam climbed the tree ; the boughs
rustled, withered, behind them ; they saw
the secluded vision of battle in the law ;
they found the terror in the Emperor's house.

The tree about them died undying,
the good lusted against the good,
the Acts in conflict envenomed the blood,
on the twisted tree hung their body wrying.

Joints cramped ; a double entity
spewed and struggled, good against good ;
they saw the mind of the Emperor as they could,
his imagination of the wars of identity.

He walked slowly through his habitation
in the night of himself without him ; Byzantium slept ;
a white pulsing shape behind him crept,
the ejection to the creature of the creature's rejection of
   salvation.

Conception without control had the Adam of the error ;
stifled over their head, the tree's bright beam
lost in the sides of the pit its aerial stream ;
they had their will ; they saw ; they were torn in the terror.

θ

Elburz sinks through the Golden Horn :
the feet of creation walk backward through the waters.

The single galley hardly moves,
the stiffening mechanic of arms and oars fails ;
patched with undyed canvas the purple sails
drag at the flagging hands of man ;
the sea's unaccumulated distance drags at the sailor's hearts.

The sea-borne Asian mine,
stuff of Caucasia fashioned in Byzantium,
earth's gold sprinkled over the sea
and plated round the poop of the visionary spirit,
shines no longer nor lustily gleams.

On the brazen deck blasts of hot ashes
fall from unseen volcanoes ; harsh birds,
stabbing at sea-broods, grating their mating calls,
cover it ; down their flight gusts drove once the galley.

Phosphorescent on the stagnant level
a headless figure walks in a crimson cope,
volcanic dust blown under the moon.

A brainless form, as of the Emperor,
walks, indecent hands hidden under the cope,
dishallowing in that crimson the flush on the mounds of
    Caucasia.

His guard heaves round him ; heaven-sweeping tentacles
stretch, dragging octopus bodies over the level ;
his cope by two is lifted from his body,
where it walks on the sinking floor of antipodean Byzantium.
Let us gaze, son of man, on the Acts in contention.

Phosphorescent gleams the point of the penis :
rudiments or relics, disappearing, appearing,
live in the forlorn focus of the intellect,
eyes and ears, the turmoil of the mind of sensation.

Inarticulate always on an inarticulate sea
beyond P'o-lu the headless Emperor moves,
the octopuses round him ; lost are the Roman hands ;
lost are the substantial instruments of being.

The organic body sang together ;
the Acts of identity adored their Lord ;
the song sprang and rang in Byzantium.

O you shoulders, elbows, wrists,
bless him, praise him, magnify him for ever ;
you fittings of thumbs and fingers,
bless ye the Lord ;

sockets and balls in knees and ankles,
bless ye the Lord ;
hips, thighs, spine in its multiples,
bless him, praise him, magnify him for ever ;
bless him in Caucasia, bless him in Lateran,
bless him in the blazons of London-in-Logres,
if there be worlds of language beyond Logres,
bless him, praise him, magnify him for ever ;
if there be wit in the rolling mass of waters,
if any regimen in marshes beyond P'o-lu,
if any measurement among the headless places,
bless him, praise him, magnify him for ever.

The Calling of Arthur

Arthur was young ; Merlin met him on the road.
  Wolfish, the wizard stared, coming from the wild,
  black with hair, bleak with hunger, defiled
from a bed in the dung of cattle, inhuman his eyes.

Bold stood Arthur ; the snow beat ; Merlin spoke :
  Now am I Camelot ; now am I to be builded.
  King Cradlemas sits by Thames ; a mask o'ergilded
covers his wrinkled face, all but one eye.

Cold and small he settles his rump in the cushions.
  Through the emerald of Nero one short-sighted eye
  peers at the pedlars of wealth that stand plausibly by.
The bleak mask is gilded with a maiden's motionless smile.

The high aged voice squeals with callous comfort.
  He sits on the bank of Thames, a sea-snail's shell
  fragile, fragilely carved, cast out by the swell
on to the mud ; his spirit withers and dies.

He withers ; he peers at the tide ; he squeals.
  He warms himself by the fire and eats his food
  through a maiden's motionless mouth ; in his mood
he polishes his emerald, misty with tears for the poor.

The waste of snow covers the waste of thorn ;
  on the waste of hovels snow falls from a dreary sky ;
  mallet and scythe are silent ; the children die.
King Cradlemas fears that the winter is hard for the poor.

The Calling of Arthur

Draw now the tide, spring moon, swing now the depth ;
   under the snow that falls over brick and prickle,
   the people ebb ; draw up the hammer and sickle.
The banner of Bors is abroad ; where is the king ?

Bors is up ; his wife Elayne behind him
   mends the farms, gets food from Gaul ; the south
   is up with hammer and sickle, and holds Thames mouth.
Lancelot hastens, coming with wagons and ships.

The sea-snail lies by Thames ; O wave of Pendragon,
   roll it, swallow it ; pull the mask o'ergilded
   from the one-eyed face that blinks at the comfort builded
in London's ruins ; I am Camelot ; Arthur, raise me.

Arthur ran ; the people marched ; in the snow
   King Cradlemas died in his litter ; a screaming few
   fled ; Merlin came ; Camelot grew.
In Logres the king's friend landed, Lancelot of Gaul.

Mount Badon

The king's poet was his captain of horse in the wars.
He rode over the ridge ; his force
sat hidden behind, as the king's mind had bidden.
The plain below held the Dragon in the centre,
Lancelot on the left, on the right Gawaine,
Bors in the rear commanding the small reserve :
the sea's indiscriminate host roared at the City's wall.
As with his household few Taliessin rode over the ridge,
the trumpets blew, the lines engaged.

Staring, motionless, he sat ;
who of the pirates saw ? none stopped ;
they cropped and lopped Logres ; they struck deep,
and their luck held ; only support lacked :
neither for charge nor for ruse could the allied crews
abide the civilized single command ;
each captain led his own band and each captain unbacked ;
but numbers crashed ; Taliessin saw Gawaine
fail, recover, and fail again ;
he saw the Dragon sway ; far away
the household of Lancelot was wholly lost in the fray ;
he saw Bors fling
company after company to the aid of the king,
till the last waited the word alone.

Staring, motionless, he sat.
Dimly behind him he heard how his staff stirred.

One said : " He dreams or makes verse " ; one : " Fool,
all lies in a passion of patience—my lord's rule."
In a passion of patience he waited the expected second.
Suddenly the noise abated, the fight vanished, the last
few belated shouts died in a new quiet.
In the silence of a distance, clear to the king's poet's sight,
Virgil was standing on a trellised path by the sea.
Taliessin saw him negligently leaning ; he felt
the deep breath dragging the depth of all dimension,
as the Roman sought for the word, sought for his thought,
sought for the invention of the City by the phrase.
He saw Virgil's unseeing eyes ; his own,
in that passion of all activity but one suspended,
leaned on those screened ports of blind courage.
Barbaric centuries away, the ghostly battle contended.

Civilized centuries away, the Roman moved.
Taliessin saw the flash of his style
dash at the wax ; he saw the hexameter spring
and the king's sword swing ; he saw, in the long field,
the point where the pirate chaos might suddenly yield,
the place for the law of grace to strike.
He stood in his stirrups ; he stretched his hand ;
he fetched the pen of his spear from its bearer ;
his staff behind signed to their men.

The Æneid's beaked lines swooped on Actium ;
the stooped horse charged ; backward blown,
the flame of song streaked the spread spears
and the strung faces of words on a strong tongue.
The household of Taliessin swung on the battle ;

hierarchs of freedom, golden candles of the solstice
that flared round the golden-girdled Logos, snowy-haired,
brazen-footed, starry-handed, the thigh banded with the
    Name.

The trumpets of the City blared through the feet of brass ;
the candles flared among the pirates ; their mass broke ;
Bors flung his company forward ; the horse and the reserve
caught the sea's host in a double curve ;
the paps of the day were golden-girdled ;
hair, bleached white by the mere stress of the glory,
drew the battle through the air up threads of light.
The tor of Badon heard the analytical word ;
the grand art mastered the thudding hammer of Thor,
and the heart of our lord Taliessin determined the war.

The lord Taliessin kneeled to the king ;
the candles of new Camelot shone through the fought field.

The Crowning of Arthur

The king stood crowned ; around in the gate,
midnight striking, torches and fires
massing the colour, casting the metal,
furnace of jubilee, through time and town,
Logres heraldically flaunted the king's state.

The lords sheathed their swords ; they camped
by Camelot's wall ; thick-tossed torches,
tall candles flared, opened, deployed ;
between them rose the beasts of the banners ;
flaring over all the king's dragon ramped.

Wars were at end ; the king's friend stood
at the king's side ; Lancelot's lion
had roared in the pattern the king's mind cherished,
in charges completing the strategy of Arthur ;
the king's brain working in Lancelot's blood.

Presaging intelligence of time climbed,
Merlin climbed, through the dome of Stephen,
over chimneys and churches ; from the point of Camelot
he looked through the depth to the dome of Sophia ;
the kingdom and the power and the glory chimed.

He turned where the fires, amid burning mail,
poured, tributaried by torches and candles,
to a point in a massive of colour, one
aureole flame ; the first shield's deep azure,
sidereally pointed, the lord Percivale.

Driving back that azure a sea rose black ;
on a fess of argent rode a red moon.
The Queen Morgause leaned from a casement ;
her forehead's moon swallowed the fires,
it was crimson on the bright-banded sable of Lamorack.

The tincture changed ; ranged the craft
of the king's new champion in a crimson field ;
mockery in mockery, a dolphin naiant ;
a silver fish under bloody waters,
conquered or conquering, Dinadan laughed.

A pelican in golden piety struck well
the triple bloody drops from its wound ;
in strong nurture of instinct, it smote
for its young its breast ; the shield of Bors
bore its rich fervours, to itself most fell.

Shouldering shapes through the skies rise and run,
through town and time ; Merlin beheld
the beasts of Broceliande, the fish of Nimue,
hierarchic, republican, the glory of Logres,
patterns of the Logos in the depth of the sun.

Taliessin in the crowd beheld the compelled brutes,
wildness formalized, images of mathematics,
star and moon, dolphin and pelican,
lion and leopard, changing their measure.
Over the mob's noise rose gushing the sound of the flutes.

Gawaine's thistle, Bedivere's rose, drew near :
flutes infiltrating the light of candles.
Through the magical sound of the fire-strewn air,
spirit, burning to sweetness of body,
exposed in the midst of its bloom the young queen Guinevere.

Lancelot moved to descend ; the king's friend kneeled,
the king's organic motion, the king's mind's blood,
the lion in the blood roaring through the mouth of creation
as the lions roar that stand in the Byzantine glory.
Guinevere's chalice flew red on an argent field.

So, in Lancelot's hand, she came through the glow,
into the king's mind, who stood to look on his city :
the king made for the kingdom, or the kingdom made for the
    king ?
Thwart drove his current against the current of Merlin :
in beleaguered Sophia they sang of the dolorous blow.

Doom in shocks sprinkled the burning gloom,
molten metals and kindling colours pouring
into the pyre ; at the zenith lion and dragon
rose, clawed, twisted, screamed ;
Taliessin beheld a god lie in his tomb.

At the door of the gloom sparks die and revive ;
the spark of Logres fades, glows, fades.
It is the first watch ; the Pope says Matins in Lateran ;
the hollow call is beaten on the board in Sophia ;
the ledge of souls shudders, whether they die or live.

Taliessin's Song of the Unicorn

Shouldering shapes of the skies of Broceliande
    are rumours in the flesh of Caucasia ; they raid the west,
clattering with shining hooves, in myth scanned—
    centaur, gryphon, but lordlier for verse is the crest
of the unicorn, the quick panting unicorn ; he will come
    to a girl's crooked finger or the sharp smell
of her clear flesh—but to her no good ; the strum
    of her blood takes no riot or quiet from the quell ;
she cannot like such a snorting alien love
    galloped from a dusky horizon it has no voice
to explain, nor the silver horn pirouetting above
    her bosom—a ghostly threat but no way to rejoice
in released satiation ; her body without delight
    chill-curdled, and the gruesome horn only to be
polished, its rifling rubbed between breasts ; right
    is the tale that a true man runs and sets the maid free,
and she lies with the gay hunter and his spear flesh-hued,
    and over their couch the spoiled head displayed—
as Lesbia tied horned Catullus—of the cuckold of the
    wood ;
such, west from Caucasia, is the will of every maid ;
    yet if any, having the cunning to call the grand beast,
the animal which is but a shade till it starts to run,
    should dare set palms on the point, twisting from the least
to feel the sharper impress, for the thrust to stun
    her arteries into channels of tears beyond blood
    (O twy-fount, crystal in crimson, of the Word's side),

Taliessin's Song of the Unicorn

and she to a background of dark bark, where the wood
    becomes one giant tree, were pinned, and plied
through hands to heart by the horn's longing : O she
    translucent, planted with virtues, lit by throes,
should be called the Mother of the Unicorn's Voice, men see
    her with awe, her son the new sound that goes
surrounding the City's reach, the sound of enskied
    shouldering shapes, and there each science disposed,
horn-sharp, blood-deep, ocean and lightning wide,
    in her paramour's song, by intellectual nuptials unclosed.

Bors to Elayne: The Fish of Broceliande

The king is building Camelot; he has bidden his host
depart to their homes, the wards only of the towns
pricked for weapons; and each lord to his own land.

He has sent me to be his lieutenant on the southern coast,
over ships in the harbours and sheep flocks on the downs;
to define the kingdom—from unpathed Broceliande

to the eastern forelands. In the great hall's glow
Taliessin sang of the sea-rooted western wood;
his song meant all things to all men, and you to me.

A forest of the creatures: was it of you? no?
monstrous beasts in the trees, birds flying the flood,
and I plucked a fish from a stream that flowed to that sea:

from you? for you? shall I drop the fish in your hand?
in your hand's pool? a bright-scaled, red-tailed fish
to dart and drive up the channel of your arm?

the channel of your arm, the piercing entry to a land
where, no matter how lordly at home is set the dish,
no net can catch it, nor hook nor gaff harm?

but it darts up the muscles of the arm, to swim
round the clear boulder of the shoulder, stung with spray,
and down the cataract of the backed spine leaps

into bottomed waters at once clear and dim,
where nets are fingered and flung on many a day ;
yet it slides through the mesh of the mind and sweeps

back to its haunt in a fathomless bottomless pool ;
is there a name then, an anagram of spirit and sense,
that Nimue the mistress of the wood could call it by ?

None but a zany, none but earth's worst fool,
could suppose he knows ; no name was thrown thence ;
some say a twy-nature only can utter the cry

(what ? how?) to bring it from the stirred stream,
and if—inhumanly flashing a sudden scale,
aboriginally shaking the aboriginal main.

Double tracks then their dazzled eyes seem
to follow : one, where the forked dominant tail
flicks, beats, reddens the smooth plane

of the happy flesh ; one, where the Catacomb's stone
holds its diagram over the happy dead
who flashed in living will through the liquid wish.

Will you open your hand now to catch your own
nova creatura ? through stream and cataract sped,
through shallow and depth ? *accipe*, take the fish.

Take ; I have seen the branches of Broceliande.
Though Camelot is built, though the king sit on the throne,
yet the wood in the wild west of the shapes and names

probes everywhere through the frontier of head and hand ;
everywhere the light through the great leaves is blown
on your substantial flesh, and everywhere your glory frames.

Taliessin in the School of the Poets

Through Camelot, which is London-in-Logres,
  by Paul's and Arthur's door,
Taliessin came to the school of the poets ;
through an exposition of song,
over a glamour of golden-work,
  his shadow fell on the floor.

Phœbus there in mid-mosaic
  on a mud-born Python trod ;
his beams about him enmeshed the world,
London, Rome, and the underseas ;
the moving shadow over all
  lapped the edge of the god.

Dusk deepened in the work's width ;
  from rituals and prophecies,
from skins of runes and vellums of verse,
the children of song to the brass of a man,
searching the dark of Phœbus' style,
  turned attentive eyes.

Their hearts ached, their thoughts toiled,
  with sorrows and young loves ;
within verse they were teased by verse ;
Taliessin stood by the chair of the poets ;
in the court beyond the lattice
  cooed the king's doves.

Butterfly fancies hovered
  round the edged Phœbean shape.
' Fortune befall,' the king's poet said,
' the weighed gold of butterflies' wings,
the measure of the swaying hazel's shade,
  or of light in the neck's nape.

' Skeined be the creamed-with-crimson sphere
  on a guessed and given line,
skeined and swirled on the head-to-heel,
or the radial arms' point-to-point ;
reckoned the rondures of the base
  by the straight absolute spine.

' Swung be the measuring hazel wand
  over thighs and shoulders bare,
and grace-pricked to gules the field
by the intinctured heart's steel ;
but best they fathom the blossom
  who fly the porphyry stair.

' At the huge and heavy stair's head
  all measures, to infinite strength,
from sapphire-laced distances drawn,
fill the jewel-joint-justiced throne ;
adored be God and the Emperor
  for the gathering of the nth.

' From the indulged Byzantine floor
  between right and left newel
floats the magnanimous path of the stair

to a tangle of compensations,
every joint a centre,
  and every centre a jewel.

' Each moment there is the midmost
  of the whole massive load ;
impulse a grace and wonder a will,
love desert, and sight direction,
whence the Acts of Identity issue
  in the Pandects and the Code ;

' while in the opposite shires of Logres
  the willows of the brook sway
by the tribal tracks and the Roman roads
in the haze of the levels and the lengthening lines,
and the nuts of the uncut hazel fall
  down the cut hazel's way.'

Taliessin's voice sharpened
  on Virgil's exact word ;
he uttered Italy seen from a wave ;
he defined the organisms of hell.
Blindfold on their perches
  the king's falcons stirred.

The darkened glamour of the golden-work
  took colour from each line ;
dimly the gazing postulants saw
patterns of multilinear red
sprinkled and spreading everywhere,
  and spaced to one design.

The king's poet stood by the sovereign chair;
  in a harsh voice he cried
of the stemming and staling of great verse,
of poetry plunged into the void
where Virgil clutched at clumps of song
  when that master of poets died.

Tendebantque manus—there
  in the broad Phœbean ground
they saw the macrocosm drawn;
they heard the universal sigh
in the balance of changing levels
  and complemented sound.

Infinite patterns opened
  in the sovereign chair's mass;
but the crowned form of anatomized man,
bones, nerves, sinews,
the diagram of the style of the Logos,
  rose in the crimson brass.

Breathless explorers of the image,
  innocent, lucent-eyed,
the young poets studied precision;
Taliessin remembered the soul:
Sis salvator, Domine,
  the king's poet sighed.

Taliessin on the Death of Virgil

Virgil fell from the edge of the world,
hurled by the thrust of Augustus' back ; the shape
he loved grew huge and black, loomed and pushed.
The air rushed up ; he fell
into despair, into air's other.
The hexameter's fullness now could find no ground ;
his mind, dizzily replete with the meaningless sweet sound,
could found no Rome there on the joys of a noise.
He fell through his moment's infinity
(no man escapes), all the shapes of his labour,
his infinite images, dropping pell-mell ; above,
loomed the gruesome great buttocks of Augustus his love,
his neighbour, infinitely large, infinitely small.
In the midst of his fall others came, none to save.
While he was dropping they put him in a grave.
Perpetual falling, perpetual burying,
this was the truth of his Charon's ferrying—
everlastingly plucked from and sucked from and plucked to
        and sucked to a grave.

Unborn pieties lived.
Out of the infinity of time to that moment's infinity
they lived, they rushed, they dived below him, they rose
to close with his fall ; all, while man is, that could
live, and would, by his hexameters, found
there the ground of their power, and their power's use.
Others he saved ; himself he could not save.

In that hour they came ; more and faster, they sped
to their dead master ; they sought him to save
from the spectral grave and the endless falling,
who had heard, for their own instruction, the sound of his
    calling.
There was intervention, suspension, the net of their loves,
all their throng's songs :
Virgil, master and friend,
holy poet, priest, president of priests,
prince long since of all our energies' end,
deign to accept adoration, and what salvation
may reign here by us, deign of goodwill to endure,
in this net of obedient loves, doves of your cote and wings,
Virgil, friend, lover, and lord.

Virgil was fathered of his friends.
He lived in their ends.
He was set on the marble of exchange.

The Coming of Palomides

Talaat ibn Kula of Ispahan
taught me the measurement of man
that Euclid and Archimedes showed,
ere I took the Western road
across the strait of the Spanish seas.
Through the green-pennon-skirted Pyrenees,
from the sharp curved line of the Prophet's blade
that cuts the Obedience from the Obeyed,
I came to the cross-littered land of Gaul.
Gospels trigonometrical
measured the height of God-in-man
by the swinging hazels of Lateran
on the hill where Cœlius Vibenna's lamp
twinkled amid the sorcerers' camp
when the Etruscan spells were thrown
over flesh and over bone,
to prevent the City and the See
by the twisted malice of Goetry.
Earth shattered under them, but therethrough
Cæsar rose and the Gospel grew,
till, lit at the star of God-in-man,
burned the candles of Lateran.
But between the magic and the mystery
Julius Cæsar heard of the sea
where trembling fishers are called to row
shadowy-cargoed boats, and know
friction of keels on the soundless coasts.

Julius pierced through the tale of ghosts,
and opened the harbours of the north.
I too from Portius Iccus forth
sailing came to the Logrian land :
there I saw an outstretched hand.

In the summer-house of the Cornish king
I kneeled to Mark at a banqueting,
I saw the hand of the queen Iseult ;
down her arm a ruddy bolt
fired the tinder of my brain
to measure the shape of man again ;
I heard the king say : ' Little we know
of verses here ; let the stranger show
a trick of the Persian music-craft.'
Iseult smiled and Tristram laughed.
Her arm exposed on the board, between
Mark and Tristram sat the queen,
but neither Mark nor Tristram sought
the passion of substantial thought,
neither Mark nor Tristram heard
the accent of the antique word.
Only the uncrossed Saracen
sang amid the heavy Cornish men ;
only, a folly amid fighting lords,
I caught her arm in a mesh of chords,
and the speech of Moslem Ispahan
swung the hazels of Lateran.

Blessed (I sang) the Cornish queen ;
for till to-day no eyes have seen
how curves of golden life define

the straightness of a perfect line,
till the queen's blessed arm became
a rigid bar of golden flame
where well might Archimedes prove
the doctrine of Euclidean love,
and draw his demonstrations right
against the unmathematic night
of ignorance and indolence !
Did, to this new-awakened sense,
he or some greater Master sweep
his compass ? fiery circles leap
round finger-point and shoulder ; arc
with arc encountering strikes a spark
wherefrom the dropping chords of fire
fashion the diagram of desire.
There flames my heart, there flames my thought,
either to double points is caught ;
lo, on the arm's base for a sign,
the single equilateral trine !

Blessed for ever be the hour
when first the intellectual power
saw triple angles, triple sides,
and that proceed which naught divides
through their great centre, by the stress
of the queen's arm's blissful nakedness,
to unions metaphysical ;
blessed the unity of all
authorities of blood and brain,
triply obedient, each to twain,
obedience in the mind, subdued

to fire of fact and fire of blood ;
obedience in the blood, exact
to fire of mind and fire of fact ;
to mind and blood the fact's intense
incredible obedience,
in the true equilateral ease.

And O what long isosceles
from finger-point and shoulder flies
towards me, and distant strain my eyes
along the twin roads, there to prove
the doctrine of Euclidean love ;
let the queen's grace but yield her hand
to be by such strong measure spanned——

In the summer house of the Cornish king
suddenly I ceased to sing.
Down the arm of the queen Iseult
quivered and darkened an angry bolt ;
and, as it passed, away and through
and above her hand the sign withdrew.
Fiery, small, and far aloof,
a tangled star in the cedar roof,
it hung ; division stretched between
the queen's identity and the queen.
Relation vanished, though beauty stayed ;
too long my dangerous eyes delayed
at the shape on the board, but voice was mute ;
the queen's arm lay there destitute,
empty of glory ; and while the king
tossed the Saracen lord a ring,

and the queen's pleasure, smiling still,
turned to Tristram's plausible skill,
three lines in a golden distance shone,
three points pricked golden and were gone.
Tristram murmured by Iseult's head.

Cœlius Vibenna over the dead
cast the foul Chthonian spells,
on ghost and bone and what lingers else ;
Cæsar heard of the ghostly sea
that masks the ports of the unity ;
the Pope in white, like the ghost of man,
stood in the porch of Lateran ;
and aloof in the roof, beyond the feast,
I heard the squeak of the questing beast,
where it scratched itself in the blank between
the queen's substance and the queen.

Lamorack and the Queen Morgause of Orkney

Hued from the livid everlasting stone
the queen's hewn eyelids bruised my bone ;
my eyes splintered, as our father Adam's when the first
exorbitant flying nature round creation's flank burst.

Her hair was whirlwind about her face ;
her face outstripped her hair ; it rose from a place
where pre-Adamic sculpture on an ocean rock lay,
and the sculpture torn from its rock was swept away.

Her hand discharged catastrophe ; I was thrown
before it ; I saw the source of all stone,
the rigid tornado, the schism and first strife
of primeval rock with itself, Morgause Lot's wife.

I had gone in summer at the king's word to explore
the coast of the kingdom towards the Pole ; the roar
of the ocean beyond all coasts threatened on one hand ;
on the other we saw the cliffs of Orkney stand.

Caves and hollows in the crags were filled with the scream
of seamews nesting and fleeting ; the extreme theme
of Logres rose in harsh cries and hungry storms,
and there, hewn in a cleft, were hideous huge forms.

I remembered how the archbishop in Caerleon at a feast
preached that before the making of man or beast
the Emperor knew all carved contingent shapes
in torrid marsh temples or on cold crookt capes.

These were the shapes only the Emperor knew,
unless Cœlius Vibenna and his loathly few,
squat by their pot, by the twisted hazel art
sought the image of that image within their heart.

Sideways in the cleft they lay, and the seamews' wings
everywhere flying, or the mist, or the mere slant of the things
seemed to stir them ; then the edge of the storm's shock
over us obliquely split rock from rock.

Ship and sculpture shuddered ; the crags' scream
mingled with the seamews' ; Logres' convulsed theme
wailed in the whirlwind ; we fled before the storms,
and behind us loosed in the air flew giant inhuman forms.

When from the sea I came again to my stall
King Arthur between two queens sat in a grim hall,
Guinevere on his right, Morgause on his left ;
I saw in her long eyes the humanized shapes of the cleft.

She sat the sister of Arthur, the wife of Lot,
four sons got by him, and one not.
I heard as she stirred the seamews scream again
in the envy of the unborn bastard and the pride of canonical
    Gawaine.

I turned my eyes to the lords ; they sat half-dead.
The young wizard Merlin, standing by me, said :
' Balin had Balan's face, and Morgause her brother's.
Did you not know the blow that darkened each from other's ?

' Balin and Balan fell by mistaken impious hate.
Arthur tossed loves with a woman and split his fate.
Did you not see, by the dolorous blow's might,
the contingent knowledge of the Emperor floating into sight ?

' Over Camelot and Carbonek a whirling creature hovered
as over the Adam in Eden when they found themselves
        uncovered,
when they would know good as evil ; thereon it was showed,
but then they must know God also after that mode.'

The eyes of the queen Morgause were a dark cavern ;
there a crowned man without eyes came to a carved tavern,
a wine-wide cell, an open grave, that stood
between Caerleon and Carbonek, in the skirts of the blind
        wood.

Through the rectangular door the crowned shape went its
        way ;
it lifted light feet : an eyeless woman lay
flat on the rock ; her arm was stretched to embrace
his own stretched arm ; she had his own face.

The shape of a blind woman under the shape of a blind man :
over them, half-formed, the cipher of the Great Ban,
this, below them both, the shape of the blatant beast matched ;
his mouth was open in a yelp ; his feet scratched.

Beyond them a single figure was cut in the rock;
it was hewn in a gyration of mow and mock;
it had a weasel's head and claws on hand and feet;
it twirled under an arch that gave on the city's street.

The child lies unborn in the queen's womb;
unformed in his brain is the web of all our doom,
as unformed in the minds of all the great lords
lies the image of the split Table and of surreptitious swords.

I am the queen's servant; while I live
down my eyes the cliff, the carving, the winged things drive,
since the rock, in those fleet lids of rock's hue,
the sculpture, the living sculpture, rose and flew.

Bors to Elayne: on the King's Coins

I came in ; I saw you stand,
in your hand the bread of love, in your head lightness of law.
The uprightness of the multitude stood in your figure ;
my fieldsmen ate and your women served,
while you watched them from the high seat.
When you saw me a southern burst of love
tossed a new smile from your eyes to your mouth,
shaping for that wind's while the corn of your face.
It was said once that your hair was the colour of corn ;
he who said so was capable only to adorn
the margin of parchments drawn in schools of Gaul ;
their doctrine is your hands' main. I am come again
to live from the founts and fields of your hands ;
colour is art, but my heart counts the doctrine.

On the forms of ancient saints, my heroes, your thumbs,
as on a winch the power of man is wound
to the last inch ; there ground is prepared
for the eared and seeded harvest of propinquant goodwill,
drained the reeded marches, cleared the branched jungles
where the unthumbed shapes of apes swung and hung.
Now when the thumbs are muscled with the power of good-
    will
corn comes to the mill and the flour to the house,
bread of love for your women and my men ;
at the turn of the day, and none only to earn ;
in the day of the turn, and none only to pay ;

Bors to Elayne: on the King's Coins

for the hall is raised to the power of exchange of all
by the small spread organisms of your hands; O Fair,
there are the altars of Christ the City extended.
I have ridden all night from organization in London,
ration and rule, and the fault in ration and rule,
law and the flaw in law, to reach to you,
the sole figure of the organic salvation of our good.

The king has set up his mint by Thames.
He has struck coins; his dragon's loins
germinate a crowded creaturely brood
to scuttle and scurry between towns and towns,
to furnish dishes and flagons with change of food;
small crowns, small dragons, hurry to the markets
under the king's smile, or flat in houses squat.
The long file of their snouts crosses the empire,
and the other themes acknowledge our king's head.
They carry on their backs little packs of value,
caravans; but I dreamed the head of a dead king
was carried on all, that they teemed on house-roofs
where men stared and studied them as I your thumbs'
    epigrams,
hearing the City say *Feed my lambs*
to you and the king; the king can tame dragons to carriers,
but I came through the night, and saw the dragonlets'
    eyes
leer and peer, and the house-roofs under their weight
creak and break; shadows of great forms
halloed them on, and followed over falling towns.
I saw that this was the true end of our making;
mother of children, redeem the new law.

They laid the coins before the council.
Kay, the king's steward, wise in economics, said :
' Good ; these cover the years and the miles
and talk one style's dialects to London and Omsk.
Traffic can hold now and treasure be held,
streams are bridged and mountains of ridged space
tunnelled ; gold dances deftly across frontiers.
The poor have choice of purchase, the rich of rents,
and events move now in a smoother control
than the swords of lords or the orisons of nuns.
Money is the medium of exchange.'

Taliessin's look darkened ; his hand shook
while he touched the dragons ; he said ' We had a good
    thought.
Sir, if you made verse you would doubt symbols.
I am afraid of the little loosed dragons.
When the means are autonomous, they are deadly ; when
    words
escape from verse they hurry to rape souls ;
when sensation slips from intellect, expect the tyrant ;
the brood of carriers levels the good they carry.
We have taught our images to be free ; are we glad ?
are we glad to have brought convenient heresy to Logres ?'

The Archbishop answered the lords ;
his words went up through a slope of calm air :
' Might may take symbols and folly make treasure,
and greed bid God, who hides himself for man's pleasure
by occasion, hide himself essentially : this abides—
that the everlasting house the soul discovers

is always another's ; we must lose our own ends ;
we must always live in the habitation of our lovers,
my friend's shelter for me, mine for him.
This is the way of this world in the day of that other's ;
make yourselves friends by means of the riches of iniquity,
for the wealth of the self is the health of the self exchanged.
What saith Heracleitus ?—and what is the City's breath ?—
dying each other's life, living each other's death.
Money is a medium of exchange.'

I have come now to kiss each magnanimous thumb,
muscles of the brain, functions of the City.
I was afraid the Council had turned you into gold,
as was told of Midas who had ass's ears.
What can be saved without order ? and how order ?
Compact is becoming contract ; man only earns, and pays,
the house outside the City burns but the house within is
    enslaved.
What without coinage or with coinage can be saved ?
O lady, your hand held the bread
and Christ the City spread in the extensor muscles of your
    thumbs.

Say—can the law live ?
can the dead king's head live ?
Pray, mother of children, pray for the coins,
pray for Camelot, pray for the king, pray.

The Star of Percivale

By the magical western door in the king's hall
the Lord Percivale harped ; he added no voice ;
between string and string, all accumulated distance of sound,
a star rode by, through the round window, in the sky of
    Camelot.

Taliessin stood in the court ; he played
a borrowed harp ; his voice defined the music.
Languid, the soul of a maid, at service in the hall,
heard, rose, ran fleetly to fall at his feet.

Soft there, quiescent in adoration, it sang :
Lord, art thou he that cometh ? take me for thine.
The music rang ; the king's poet leaned to cry :
See thou do it not ; I too am a man.

The king's poet leaned, catching the outspread hands :
More than the voice is the vision, the kingdom than the king :
the cords of their arms were bands of glory ; the harp
sang her to her feet ; sharply, sweetly, she rose.

The soul of a serving-maid stood by the king's gate,
her face flushed with the mere speed of adoration.
The Archbishop stayed, coming through the morning to the
    Mass,
Hast thou seen so soon, bright lass, the light of Christ's glory ?

She answered : *The light of another, if aught, I bear,*
as he the song of another; he said : I obey.
And Dubric : *Also thy joy I wear; shall we fail*
from Percivale's world's orbit, we there once hurled?

The sun rose, bringing cloud ;
the day-star vanished ; the king's household in the court
waited ; their voices were loud ; they talked of their fights
till the altar centred between lights ; the lords entered.

The nuntius of Byzantium there, the Emperor's logothete,
angelic, white chlamys crimson-girdled, saw in a vision
a new direct earth of sweet joy given
and its fusion with a new heaven, indirect joy of substitution.

The household kneeled ; the Lord Balin the Savage moved
restless, through-thrust with a causeless vigil of anger ;
the king in the elevation beheld and loved himself crowned ;
Lancelot's gaze at the Host found only a ghost of the Queen.

The Ascent of the Spear

Taliessin walked in the palace yard;
he saw, under a guard, a girl sit in the stocks.
The stable-slaves, lounging by the gate,
cried catcalls and mocks, flung roots and skins of fruits.
She, rigid on the hard bench, disdained
motion, her cheek stained with a bruise, veined
with fury her forehead. The guard laughed and chaffed;
when Taliessin stepped near, he leapt to a rigid salute.
Lightly the king's poet halted, took the spear
from the manned hand, and with easy eyes dismissed.
Nor wist the crowd, he gone, what to do;
lifted arms fell askew; jaws gaped;
claws of fingers uncurled. They gazed,
amazed at the world of each inflexible head.

The silence loosened to speech; the king's poet said:
'Do I come as a fool? forgive folly; once more
be kind, be faithful: did we not together adore?
Say then what trick of temper or fate?' Hard-voiced,
she said without glancing, 'I sit here for taking a stick
to a sneering bastard slut, a Mongol ape,
that mouthed me in a wrangle.
Fortunate, for a brawl in the hall, to escape,
they dare tell me, the post, the stripping and whipping:
should I care, if the hazel rods cut flesh from bone?'
'Ah lady,' the king's poet murmured, 'confess yes,
except in the stress of a sin worse than the rage.

Though the High Steward's needful law punish the flaw,
wrong not us with pride of guilt or no guilt.
Be witness, Virgil, I too have been rash
to curse the praters and graters of verse.
Engage the flash of thy pardon, Omnipotence, there !
But here before this crowd,.
do we amiss ? are we proud ? '   Burning red,
with the laugh half-sob, she said :
' We do amiss—if we——— ' : and he :
' You whose arrogant hands would not cast one skin,
beloved, will you be wroth with your own poor kin ?
Though the Caucasian theme throb with its dull ache
make, lady, the Roman motion ; undo
the fierce grasp from the bench ; lay on the spear-shaft ;
climb gently ; clasp
the massive of light, in whose point serene and severe
Venus, Percivale's planet, phosphor and hesper, is here.'
She obeyed ; she made assent and ascent :
she laid below his her hand on the shaft :
under the Direction she denied pride ;
her heart flowed to the crowd.

By Taliessin's side a demure chamberlain spoke :
' The High Steward to the king's poet : the lord Kay to the
    lord Taliessin :
if who sits here be his friend,
her fetter is his to keep or end.'
' Nor mine,' the king's poet said, ' to prefer.   Sir,
she is, of force, at hand : ask her,
and do, either way, a grace of thanks to my lord.'
The messenger glanced.   Celestialling the word,

her colour a deference still,
her voice adored and implored : ' Lord, what choice ? '
   Who :
' True ; yet if the king's servant and yours could speak,
he might hold it for heaven's best skill
to treat the world's will but as and at the world's will.'
' They will say——' she began ; and he :
'—either way ; they will use to call either side
pride (to stay) or fear (to go).
Do they—do we—know ?   Love, and do what you choose.'
She said : ' I will take the Steward's grace :
do I well ? '   ' Is it I then,' the king's poet said, ' whose face
Christ beholds now suffused and sufficed with his brilliant
   blood ?
whom the feline guile of Omnipotence lures ? '
The chamberlain with a sly smile offered the keys.
Taliessin signed them away.   ' Release ?
Let come the fellow whose duty unlocks the stocks' bar :
is it ours to undo
the fetter whereto the world's order consigned
its own disordered mind ? '

Aching, stiff, she rose, stumbled, fell ;
the king's poet caught her.   ' So are the guilty taught,
sweet friend, who sit in the pass of the Perilous Sell.'
She said, ' I was wrong from beginning——'   ' Not to an end.
O new Pheilippides, that stumble was Marathon won.
Remains but the triumph's race to run.'

The Sister of Percivale

The horizon of sensation ran north at the back of Gaul;
Taliessin lay on the wall; a bright fork
from the sky of July flicked hall and horizon.

He lay between both in a morn's mist of making;
idleness cured sloth; his voice
rove and drove words to the troth of ambiguous verse.

In the yard below him a slave's back bent to a well;
it was scarred from whip or sword; the mark
flickered white in the light; hard she swung the handle.

The scar lightened over a curved horizon,
a flash, even in daylight, beheld by heightened eyes,
over the back, a track brightened by boundary peaks.

Jura, Alp, Elburz, Gaul to Caucasia,
eastward; the hall westward cut the sky;
beyond it Percivale's duchy, Wales, and all Broceliande.

She swung from the hips; the handle hard-creaking
cut the voice of Lancelot speaking to the nuntius.
The horizon in her eyes was breaking with distant Byzantium.

Taliessin saw the curved bottom of the world;
his heart—swollen with wonder—swerved on the smooth
    slopes,
reserved always the ride through the themes and Hesper for
    guide.

A round plane of water rose shining in the sun ;
she steadied the handle, the strain ceased ; her arm
balanced the line of the spine and reached for the gain.

Taliessin, watching, played with a line : ' O
Logres centre, can we know what proportion
bear the radii so to the full circumference everywhere ? '

A trumpet's sound from the gate leapt level with the arm,
round with breath as that with flesh, to a plan
blown as that bone-patterned, bound each to a point.

The sound sprang aloft from the western gate ;
a new fate had ridden from the hidden horizon ;
its luck struck as her shoulders took the weight of the water.

In her other outflung arm the sound doubled ; she cast
one look at herself in the drawn flood and passed ;
blent as she went with the blast was the voice of Percivale.

As she at her image Taliessin at the double grace
gazed in the yard ; hemispheres altered place ;
there first and then he saw the rare face of Blanchefleur.

She stood between her brothers, the lords Percivale and
    Lamorack ;
horizon had no lack of horizon ; the circle closed ;
the face of Blanchefleur was the grace of the Back in the Mount.

Her gown was marked with a curve of gold on each breast ;
from a golden brooch the mid-gold ran down to the hem ;
the red track of the back was shown in a front of glory.

Percivale saw his verse-brother lying alone,
rapt on the just glory of the sacred Throne,
the lore of the Emperor patterned in the blast and bone.

Percivale called, saying : ' Sir, speak ;
or is the king's poet weak from Caucasian journeys ?
does the stress of the Empire tire the study of Greek
    minuscula ? '

Taliessin leapt from the wall to greet the princess,
saying : ' Bless me, transit of Venus ! '
The stress of the scar ran level with the star of Percivale.

' Scars and lightnings are the edge of the spun wheel ;
spun is the reel to the height ; the plane revolves ;
the peal breaks from the bone and the way of union speaks.

' Blessed is the eyed axis of both horizons,
and the wheel that taxes the hips and generates the sphere,
and illumination that waxes in the full revolution.'

Proportion of circle to diameter, and the near asymptote
Blanchefleur's smile ; there in the throat her greeting
sprang, and sang in one note the infinite decimal.

The Son of Lancelot

The Lupercalia danced on the Palatine
among women thrusting under the thong ; vicars
of Rhea Silvia, vestal, Æneid, Mars-seeded,
mother of Rome ; they exulted in the wolf-month.
The Pope's eyes were glazed with terror of the Mass ;
his voice shook on Lateran, saying the Confiteor.
Over Europe and beyond Camelot the wolves ranged.

Rods of divination between Lupercal and Lateran :
at the height of the thin night air of Quinquagesima,
in Camelot, in the chamber of union, Merlin dissolved
the window of horny sight on a magical ingress ;
with the hazel of ceremony, fetched to his hand—cut,
smoothed, balsamed with spells, blessed with incision—
he struck from the body of air the anatomical
body of light ; he illustrated the high grades.
In the first circle he saw Logres and Europe
sprinkled by the red glow of brute famine
in the packed eyes of forest-emerging wolves,
heaped fires in villages, torches in towns,
lit for safety ; flat, frozen, trapped
under desecrated parallels, clawed perceptions
denounced to a net of burning plunging eyes,
earth lay, at the knots the protective fires ;
and he there, in his own point of Camelot,
of squat snow houses and huddled guards.

Along the print of the straight and sacred hazel
he sent his seeing into the second sphere :
to the images of accumulated distance, tidal figures
shaped at the variable climax of temperatures ; the king
dreaming of a red Grail in an ivory Logres
set for wonder, and himself Byzantium's rival
for men's thuribled and throated worship—magic
throws no truck with dreams ; the rod thrust by :
Taliessin beneath the candles reading from Bors
letters how the Moslem hunt in the Narrow Seas
altogether harried God and the soul out of flesh,
and plotting against the stresses of sea and air
the building of a fleet, and the burning blazon-royal
flying on a white field in the night—the hazel
drove, slowly humming, through spirals of speculation,
and Merlin saw, on the circle's yonder edge,
Blanchefleur, Percivale's sister, professed at Almesbury
to the nuns of infinite adoration, veiled
passions, sororal intellects, earth's lambs,
wolves of the heavens, heat's pallor's secret
within and beyond cold's pallor, fires
lit at Almesbury, at Verulam, at Canterbury, at Lateran,
and she the porter, she the contact of exchange.

Merlin grew rigid ; down the implacable hazel
(a scar on a slave, a verse in Virgil, the reach
of an arm to a sickle, love's means to love)
he sent his hearing into the third sphere—
once by a northern poet beyond Snowdon
seen at the rising of the moon, the *mens sensitiva,*

the feeling intellect, the prime and vital principle,
the pattern in heaven of Nimue, time's mother on earth,
Broceliande. Convection's tides cease
there, temperature is steady to all tenderness
in the last reach of the hazel; fixed is the full.
He knew distinction in three abstractions of sound,
the women's cry under the thong of Lupercal,
the Pope's voice singing the Glory on Lateran,
the howl of a wolf in the coast of Broceliande.
The notes of Lupercal and Lateran ceased; fast
Merlin followed his hearing down the wolf's howl
back into sight's tritosphere—thence was Carbonek
prodigiously besieged by a feral famine; a single
wolf, grey and gaunt, that had been Lancelot,
imbruted, watching the dark unwardened arch,
crouched on the frozen snow beyond Broceliande.

Pelles the Wounded King lay in Carbonek,
bound by the grating pain of the dolorous blow;
his flesh from dawn-star to noontide day by day
ran as a woman's under the moon; in midsun
he called on the reckless heart of God and the Emperor;
he commended to them and commanded himself and his
    land.
Now in the wolf-month nine moons had waned
since Lancelot, ridden on a merciful errand, came
that night to the house; there, drugged and blurred
by the medicated drink of Brisen, Merlin's sister,
he lay with the princess Helayne, supposed Guinevere.
In the morning he saw; he sprang from the tall window;

he ran into a delirium of lycanthropy ; he grew
backward all summer, laired in the heavy wood.
In autumn King Pelles' servants brought him news
of a shape glimpsed on the edge of Broceliande,
a fear in the forest, a foe by the women's well.

Patient, the king constrained patience, and bade
wait till the destined mother's pregnancy was done.
All the winter the wolf haunted the environs of Carbonek ;
now what was left of the man's contrarious mind
was twinned and twined with the beast's bent to feed ;
now it crept to swallow the seed
of love's ambiguity, love's taunt and truth.
Man, he hated ; beast, he hungered ; both
stretched his sabres and strained his throat ; rumble
of memories of love in the gaunt belly told
his instinct only that something edible might come.
Slavering he crouched by the dark arch of Carbonek,
head-high howling, lusting for food, living
for flesh, a child's flesh, his son's flesh.

And infinite beyond him the whole Empire contracted
from (within it) wolves, and (without it) Moslems.
The themes fell back round separate defensive fires ;
there only warmth dilated ; there they circled.
Caucasia was lost, Gaul was ravaged, Jerusalem
threatened ; the crescent cut the Narrow Seas,
while from Cordovan pulpits the iconoclastic
heretical licentiates of Manes denounced union,
and only Lupercal and Lateran preserved Byzantium.

Helayne, Lancelot's bed-fellow, felt her labour.
Brisen knelt ; Merlin watched her hands ;
the children of Nimue timed and spaced the birth.
Contraction and dilation seized the substance of joy,
the body of the princess, but in her stayed from terror,
from surplus of pain, from outrage, from the wolf in
    flesh,
such as racked in a cave the Mother of Lupercal
and now everywhere the dilating and contracting Empire.
The child slid into space, into Brisen's hands.
Polished brown as hazel-nuts his eyes
opened on his foster-mother ; he smiled at space.
Merlin from the hazel's divination saw
the child lie in his sister's hands ; he saw
over the Empire the lucid flash of all flesh,
shining white on the sullen white of the snow.
He ran down the hazel ; he closed the window ; he
    came
past the royal doors of dream, where Arthur, pleased
with the Grail cooped for gustation and God for his glory,
the æsthetic climax of Logres, softly slept ;
but the queen's tormented unæsthetic womanhood
alternately wept and woke, her sobs crushed
deep as the winter howls were high, her limbs
swathed by tentacles, her breasts sea-weighed.
Across the flat sea she saw Lancelot
walking, a grotesque back, the opposite of a face
looking backward like a face ; she burst the swollen sea
shrieking his name ; nor he turned nor looked,
but small on the level dwindled to a distant manikin,
the tinier the more terrible, the sole change

in her everlastingness, except, as Merlin passed,
once as time passed, the hoary waters
laughed backward in her mouth and drowned her tongue.

Through London-in-Logres Merlin came to the wall,
the soldiers saw him ; their spears clapped.
For a blade's flash he smiled and blessed their guard,
and went through the gate, beyond the stars' spikes—
as beyond palisades to everywhere the plunging fires,
as from the *mens sensitiva*, the immortal tenderness,
magically exhibited in the ceremonial arts,
to the raging eyes, the rearing bodies, the red
carnivorous violation of intellectual love,
and the frozen earth whereon they ran and starved.
Far as Lancelot's dwindling back from the dumb
queen in a nightmare of the flat fleering ocean,
the soldiers saw him stand, and heard as if near—
far to sight, near to sound—the small
whistling breath in the thin air of Quinquagesima
of the incantation, the manner of the second working.
Then the tall form on the frozen snow
dilated to monstrosity, swelling as if power
entered it visibly, from all points of the wide
sky of the wolf-month : the shape lurched and fell,
dropping on all fours, lurched and leapt and ran,
a loping terror, hurtling over the snow,
a giant white wolf, diminishing with distance,
till only to their aching eyes a white atom
spiralled wildly on the white earth, and at last
was lost ; there the dark horizontal edge
of a forest closed their bleak world.

Between the copses on the coast of Broceliande
galloped the great beast, the fierce figure
of universal consumption, Lupercal and Lateran,
taunt of truth, love's means to love
in the wolf-hour, as to each man in each man's hour
the gratuitous grace of greed, grief, or gain,
the measure pressed and overrunning ; now the cries
were silent on Lupercal, the Pope secret on Lateran.
Brisen in Helayne's chamber heard the howl
of Lancelot, and beyond it the longer howl of the air
that gave itself up in Merlin ; she felt him come.
She rose, holding the child ; the wolf and the other,
the wind of the magical wintry beast, broke
together on her ears ; the child's mouth opened ;
his wail was a song and a sound in the third heaven.
Down the stair of Carbonek she came to the arch
and paused beneath ; the wolf's hair rose on his hackles.
He dragged his body nearer ; he was hungry for his son.

The Emperor in Byzantium nodded to the exarchs ;
it was night still when the army began to move,
embarking, disembarking, before dawn Asia
awoke to hear the songs, the shouts, the wheels
of the furnished lorries rolling on the roads to the east,
and the foremost outposts of mountaineers scanning
the mouths of the caves in snowy Elburz, where hid
the hungry Christian refugees, their land
wholly abandoned to beast and Manichæan :
the city on the march to renew the allegiance of
     Caucasia.

A white wolf drove down the wood's path,
flying on the tender knowledge of the third heaven
out into moonlight and Brisen's grey eyes.
She called : ' Be blessed, brother ' ; the child sang :
' blessed brother,' and nestled to its first sleep.
Merlin broke from the wood and crouched to the leap ;
the father of Galahad smelt his coming ; he turned,
swerving from his hunger to the new danger, and
    sprang.
The driving shoulder of Merlin struck him in mid-air
and full the force of the worlds. flung ; helpless
he was twisted and tossed in vacancy ; nine yards off
the falling head of Lancelot struck the ground.
Senseless he lay ; lined in the lupine shape,
dimly, half-man, half-beast, was Lancelot's form.
Brisen ran ; with wrappings of crimson wool
she bound the child to her crouching brother's back ;
kissed them both, and dismissed ; small and asleep,
and warm on a wolf's back, the High Prince rode into
    Logres.

Blanchefleur sat at Almesbury gate ; the sleeping
sisters preserved a dreamless adoration.
Blanchefleur prayed for Percivale and Taliessin,
lords in her heart, brothers in the grand art,
exchanging tokens ; for the king and queen ; for Lancelot
nine months lost to Logres ; for the house-slaves
along whose sinewy sides the wolf-cubs leapt,
played in their hands, laired in their eyes, romped
in the wrestle of arms and thighs, cubs of convection,

haggard but held in the leash, foster-children
of the City, foster-fellows of the Merciful Child.
Suddenly, as far off as Blanchefleur deep
in exchange with the world, love's means to love,
she saw on the clear horizon an atom, moving,
waxing, white in white, speed in snow,
a silver shape in the moonlight changing to crimson,
a line of launched glory.

                      The child of Nimue
came, carrying the child of grace in flesh,
truth and taunt inward and outward ; fast
Merlin ran through Logres in the wolf-month
before spring and the leaf-buds in the hazel-twigs.
Percivale's sister rose to her feet ; her key
turned, and Almesbury gate opened ; she called :
' Sister,' but the white wolf lay before her ; alone
she loosened the crimson wrappings from the sleeping
    Galahad ;
high to her breast she held the child ; the wolf
fled, moving white upon motionless white,
the marks of his paws dark on the loosening snow,
and straight as the cross-stamped hazel in the king's house.
The bright intellects of passion gathered at the gate
to see the veiled blood in the child's tender cheeks ;
glowing as the speed in the face of the young Magian
when at dawn, laughing, he came to London-in-Logres ;
or the fire built in Carbonek's guest-chamber
where Lancelot lay tended, housed and a man,
to be by Easter healed and horsed for Logres ;

where at Easter the king's whole household
in the slanting Latin of the launched legions sang
      Gaudium multum annunciamus;
      nunc in saecula servi amamus;
      civitas dulcis aedificatur;
      quia qui amat Amor amatur.

Palomides Before his Christening

When I came out of the cave the sky had turned.
I have climbed since down a dead mountain,
over fossils of space in the petrifaction of time,
by the track at the slant-eyes' edge to the city of astrologers.

Astrologers and astronomers alike would starve here ;
the rocks are too hard to give any roots room.
No earth-shock alters the infinite smooth formation,
nor anywhere in the monstrous markings are lifting latches.

I determined, after I saw Iseult's arm,
to be someone, to trap the questing beast
that slid into Logres out of Broceliande
through the blank between the queen's meaning and the queen.

Having that honour I would consent to be christened,
I would come then to the Table on my own terms,
bringing a capture by which Christendom might profit,
which Pelles the wounded master could not recover.

But things went wrong ; Tristram knocked me sprawling
under the tender smile of Iseult ; my manhood,
chivalry, and scimitar-play learned from the Prophet,
could not gain me the accurate flash of her eyes.

Once I overthrew Lancelot by cheating at a tourney,
whence, enraged, fleeing, I was taken by pirates ;
Lancelot freed me—he rode on to Carbonek ;
Did I smile when I heard that he my saviour was mad ?

For bees buzzed down Iseult's arm in my brain ;
black gnats, whirring mosquitoes ; the cream
everywhere dissolved into a spinning cloud ;
and I thought if I caught the beast they would cease certainly.

They would vanish ; the crowd's mass of open mouths,
the City opening its mouth, would certainly swallow them.
There would be nothing but to admire the man
who had done what neither Tristram nor Lancelot did.

In the blank between the queen's meaning and the queen
first I followed my self away from the city
up a steep trail. Dinadan rode past me,
calling : ' Friend, the missing is often the catching.'

But I climbed ; I bruised my ankles on gaunt shapes,
knees, wrists, thighs ; I climbed up a back ;
my feet jarred on the repetition of shoulders ;
crevasses showed their polished slippery sides.

At other times I clambered over house-roofs,
without doors ; on their blank sides
the king's knights were flat cracks, chinks,
rubbed patches, their heads grey blobs.

At last, above them all, I came to a cave,
and a heap of twigs some traveller had left ;
I rubbed a fire and sat within ; the beast
lay at the cave's mouth ; I was glad of its company.

The fire burned awhile ; now I know
time was petrifying without. I sat and scratched.
Smoke in a greasy thickness rolled round the cave,
from flames of fierce fancy, flesh-fire-coloured.

Fire of the flesh subsided to ache of the bone ;
the smoke rolled out, faded, died ;
the beast, as the smoke thinned, had disappeared ;
starveling, I lay in bone on the cave's floor.

Bone lay loving bone it imagined near it,
bone of its hardness of longing, bone of its bone,
skeleton dreaming of skeleton where there was none.
From the cave the greasy smoke drifted slowly outward.

Skeleton dreamed of skeleton it loved to neighbour,
thigh yearning for thigh, humerus for humerus ;
by infinitesimal jerks on the cave's floor
it thrust sideways to the shining cates it imagined.

Bones grew brittle ; sinews yielded ; spirit
hated the air, the moving current that entered,
movements in the cubical plot of the cave, when smoke
emptied, and bones broke ; it was dull day.

Spirit spread in the cave, hating the air.
Bat-like, it hung to the roughness of rock ; it lay
sucking the hollow cavities, less than a bat,
in bones where once it had found a nourishing marrow.

At last the bats frightened me ; I left
my pretties ; airy currents blew my light
flimsy ash to the cave's mouth. There
was the track ; it went over the mountain to Caerleon.

The sky had turned round ; I could not think
why I should not be christened in the city of astrologers.
It was true I should look a fool before everyone ;
why not look a fool before everyone ?

The Chi-Ro is only a scratching like other scratchings ;
but in the turn of the sky the only scratching—
in a world of rock and one thing other than rock,
the small, slender, pointed, crimson beast ;

the scratching, biting, sliding, slithering thing,
whisking about in unreachable crevasses and cracks,
in cliffs and boulders ; the smooth-backed head-cocked
snout, and fat rump, and claws on the rock ;

the blatant agile beast. The lord Dinadan
laughed for joy when once I triumphed in the tourney ;
he called to the lords : ' This is his day ' ; to me :
' Catch as catch can ; but absence is a catch of the presence.

' Sir, if ever in a blank between this and that,
the sky turns on you, and the path slides
to the edge not the front of the eyes, come and be christened.
I will stand your godfather at the pool in Caerleon.'

Dull, undimensioned, I ride at last to Dinadan ;
he is the only lord without a lady ;
he fights and is not enclosed in fight ; he laughs
but he has not the honour and the irony of the court of culture.

The Coming of Galahad

In the hall all had what food they chose ;
they rose then, the king, Lancelot, the queen ;
they led the young man Galahad to Arthur's bed.
The bishops and peers, going with the royalties, made
ceremony ; they created a Rite. When he was laid,
and the order done, the lords went to their rooms.
The queen all night lay thinking of Lancelot's son.

At ·their rising the king's poet alone had gone
another way ; he took the canals of the palace,
the lower corridors, between maids and squires,
past the offices and fires of the king's kitchens,
till he came by a door cleft in a smooth wall
into the outer yards, the skied hall of the guards,
grooms, and scullions. He looked above ; he saw
through the unshuttered openings of stairs and rooms
the red flares of processional torches and candles
winding to the king's bed ; where instead
of Arthur Galahad that night should lie,
Helayne's son instead of the king's, Lancelot's
instead of Guinevere's, all taken at their word,
their professions, their oaths ; the third heaven heard
their declarations of love, and measured them the medium
        of exchange.

He stood looking up among the jakes and latrines ;
he touched his harp, low-chanting a nursery rhyme :

'Down the porphyry stair the queen's child ran;
there he played with his father's crown . . .'
A youth came up in the dark, the king's scavenger,
large-boned, fresh-coloured, flame-haired,
Gareth, a prince and a menial, the son of Morgause,
sent from Orkney and the skull-stone in the sea,
to be for cause of obedience set to the worst work.
None at Caerleon knew him but his brother Gawaine
and the king's poet who saw the profile of his mother,
in a grace of fate and a face too soon to be dead.
Hearing him now, Taliessin half-turned his head,
saying : ' Sir ? ' Gareth said, looking at the light :
' Lord, tell me of the new knight.'

Taliessin answered, sounding the strings still :
' Is it not known he is strange, being nurtured till,
men say, but yesterday, among the White Nuns,
by the sister of Percivale, the '—his harp sang—' princess
     Blanchefleur ? '

Gareth said : ' Lord, bless me with more.
Among the slaves I saw from the hall's door
over the meal a mystery sitting in the air—
a cup with a covered fitting under a saffron veil,
as of the Grail itself : what man
is this for whom the Emperor lifts the Great Ban ? '

Taliessin stayed the music ; he said :
' My lords and fathers the Druids between the hazels
touched poems in chords ; they made tell
of everywhere a double dance of a stone and a shell,
and the glittering sterile smile of the sea that pursues.'

Gareth answered : ' I heard it read from a book
by a Northern poet, and once I seemed to look
on Logres pouring like ocean after a girl
who ran in the van, and her hands before her stretched
shone—bright shell, transparent stone,
and the sea touched her, and suddenly by a wind was blown
back, and she mounted a wind and rode away,
and measurement went with her and all sound,
and I found myself weeping there like a fool.'

                                           ' To-day
the stone was fitted to the shell,' the king's poet said ;
' when my lord Sir Lancelot's son sat in the perilous sell,
if he be Sir Lancelot's ; in Logres the thing is done,
the thing I saw wherever I have gone—
in five houses, and each house double : the boughs
of the Druid oak, the cover of gay strokes in the play
of Caucasia, the parchments of Gaul, the altar-stone
in Lateran or Canterbury, the tall Byzantine hall—
O the double newels at the ground of the porphyry stair !
O there the double categories of shell and stone,
and the Acts of Identity uttered out of the Throne.'

' And I among dung and urine—am I one
with shell or stone,' Gareth asked, ' in the jakes ? '
But Taliessin : ' And what makes the City ? to-morrow
you shall be a prince of Orkney again ; to-night
abandon the degrees of Gawaine your brother ; consent
to be nothing but the shape in the gate of excrement,
while Galahad in peace and the king's protection sleeps :
question and digestion, rejection and election,
winged shapes of the Grail's officers, double

grand equality of the State, common of all lives,
common of all experience, sense and more ;
adore and repent, reject and elect. Sir,
without this alley-way how can man prefer ?
and without preference can the Grail's grace be stored ? '

A girl said suddenly beside them : ' Lord,
tell me the food you preferred——' ; and he : ' More
choice is within the working than goes before.
The good that was there—and did I well then ? yes ? '
She said : ' Yes ; yet has all food one taste ?
felicity does not alter ? ' He answered in haste :
' Felicity alters from its centre ; but I—free
to taste each alteration, and that within reach
then and there ; why change till the range twirls ? ' The girl's
eyes turned to the black palace and back.
She said : ' This morning when the Saracen prince was
        christened
dimly the lord Percivale's pentagram glistened
in the rain-dark stones of his eyes : what food there ? '

Taliessin answered : ' Five cells the world
gave me, five shells of multiple sound ;
but when I searched for the paths that joined the signs,
lines of the pentagram's frame, the houses fled
instead to undimensioned points ; their content slid
through the gate of the winged prince of the jakes ; pale
they fluttered in an empty fate ; the Child lay dead
in his own gate of growth—and what then,
lady, for you or me or the Saracen,
when the cut hazel has nothing to measure ? ' ' I have known,'

she said, with the scintillation of a grave smile,
' the hazel's stripes on my shoulders ; the blessed luck
of Logres has a sharp style, since I was caught free
from the pirate chaos savaging land and sea ;
is the shell thus also hidden in the stone ? '
' Also thus,' he said, ' if the heart fare
on what lies ever now on the board, stored
meats of love, laughter, intelligence, and prayer.
Is it thus ? ' and she : ' Who knows ?—and who does not care ?—
yet my heart's cheer may hope, if Messias please.
Is this the colour of my lord Galahad's eyes ? '

He said : ' The eyes of my lord are the measure of intensity
and his arms of action ; the hazel, Blanchefleur, he.
The clerks of the Emperor's house study the redaction
of categories into identity : so we.
Give me your hand.' Lightly she obeyed, and he
as lightly kissed : ' O office of all lights
from the king's scavenger to the king's substitute, mean
of the merciful Child, common of all rites,
winged wonder of shell and stone, here
a shoot of your own third heaven takes root in Logres.'

Gareth said : ' Lord, before the meal,
when he washed his hands, the water became phosphorescent ;
did you not see ? ' and he : ' Sanctity
common and crescent ! I have seen it flushed anew
in each motion and mode of the princess Blanchefleur ;
who walked dropping light, as all our beloved do.
It is the shell of adoration and the grand art.
But I looked rather to-night at the queen's hand

lying on her heart, and the way her eyes scanned
the unknown lord who sat in the perilous sell.
The bone of the fingers showed through the flesh ; they
    were claws
wherewith the queen's grace gripped : this was the stone
fitting itself to its echo.'
                         He turned to the gate
into the outer air ; she let cry :
' Lord, make us die as you would have us die.'

But he : ' Proofs were ; roofs were : I
what more ? creeds were ; songs were. Four
zones divide the empire from the Throne's firmament,
slanted to each cleft in each wall, with planets planted :
Mercury, thinning and thickening, thirsting to theft ;
Venus preference—though of the greatest, preference ;
O Earth between, O seen and strewn by the four !
Jupiter with a moon of irony and of defeated irony,
and Saturn circled, girdled by turned space.
The moon of irony shone on Lancelot at Carbonek,
the moon of defeated irony on Blanchefleur at Almesbury ;
her hands and head were the shell bursting from the stone
after it has bred in the stone ; she was bright with the moon's
    light
when truth sped from the taunt ; well she nurtured Galahad.
Logres is come into Jupiter ; all the zones
circle Saturn, spinning against the glory,
all the Throne's points, themes of the Empire.'

Emeralds of fire, blank to both, his eyes
were points of the Throne's foot that sank through Logres.

The Departure of Merlin

The Pope stands at Lateran's stone; man's
heart throbs from his vicarious hands.
The themes are pointed with a new device of brightness,
Trebizond with sun, Archangel with ice.

The blessing of Byzantium befriends the world's ends;
the great heretical doctors, Moslem and Manichæan,
fly; in time-spanned Camelot the Table changes;
the method of phenomena is indrawn to Broceliande.

Merlin bore Lancelot's child to a moon of white nuns,
a knot of nurture in a convent of spirits and suns;
thence in the perilous throne is the Child's moon risen,
pillars of palace and prison changed to the web of a wood.

The joyous moon waxes in the chair;
the blessed young sorcerer, a boy and less than a boy,
rose and ran, turning on the roads; he span
into the heart's simultaneity of repose.

Joseph of Nazareth, Joseph of Arimathea,
came dancing through the coeval-rooted world's idea.
They saw Merlin descending: they met him in the wood,
foster-fathers of beatitude to the foster-father of Galahad;

twin suns of womb and tomb; there no strife
is except growth from the roots, nor reaction but repose;
vigours of joy drive up; rich-ringed moments
thick in their trunks thrive, young-leaved their voices.

Moons and suns that rose in rites and runes
are come away from sequence, from rules of magic ;
here all is cause and all effect ; the laws
of Merlin's boyhood are unknown in Nimue's wood.

I saw from the deck of a galley becalmed in the seas
Merlin among the trees ; the headless form faded ;
throngs of trunks covered the volcanic waters ;
only the flat djongs float into alien P'o-Lu.

The sailors stared at the thick wood ; one,
ghastly and gaping, despaired of joy ; he yelled
for horror and leapt from the deck to the phosphorescence,
to the wreck of wisdom, the drowned last of love.

The purple sail moved in the wind of Broceliande ;
the sailors sprang to the oars ; the sea-call sang
bidding tack—near and far infinite and equal—
on the visionary ocean track to the port of Byzantium.

More than the fable of Dryads is troth to the Table
in the growth of hazel and elm, oak and bamboo ;
voice of all moments covers who hears as he goes
rich-ringed, young-leaved, monstrous trunks rejoice.

Time's president and precedent, grace ungrieved,
floating through gold-leaved lime or banked behind beech
to opaque green, through each membraned and tissued ex-
    perience
smites in simultaneity to times variously veined.

She who is Nimue, lady of lakes and seas,
articulation of limbs, accumulation of distance,
brings all natural becoming to her shape of immortal being,
as to a flash of seeing the women in the world's base.

Well has Merlin spoken the last spell,
worked the last image, gone to his own :
the moon waxes and wanes in the perilous chair,
where time's foster-child sits, Lancelot's son.

The Death of Palomides

Air strives with wings, wings with air.
In the space of the glory the stresses of power contend;
through the kingdom my heart's revolutions ascribe to the
    power
quicken the backward wings of passages and paths.

Once, when the Prophet's shout had taken Cordova,
north I rode through a moon of Spanish winter,
and lay for a night in a lodging of ancient Israel,
twins of Levi, under the height of Monsalvat.

Sea-grey was one and sea-wrinkled,
one burned sun-black, with clawed hands;
guttural, across the charcoal fire, their chant
dropped into pauses, poured into channelled names.

The first mathematics of Ispahan trembled
before the intoned formulæ; their smiles cast
totals from a myriad intricate calculations,
while the screams of eagles in conflict shook the Sierras.

I sat and heard, aloof in my young seed-mail,
scornful of my secret attention; the hut shook,
the air span, with titles of cherubim and seraphim;
the voices rose into clearness; they pronounced *Netzach*.

The Death of Palomides

Sharply I shouted into the sound : *Netzach ?*
What is Netzach ? Together and deeply they answered :
Netzach is the name of the Victory in the Blessing :
For the Lord created all things by means of his Blessing.

One now, sea-grey and wave-wrinkled,
calls through all my body to the sun-blackened :
The Lord created all things by means of his Blessing,
and they float upwards ; the paths open between.

Once the paths were interminable ; paths were stations.
Unangelical speed loitered upon them,
supposing the everlasting habitations had received it ;
only the dolphin Dinadan swam and smiled.

Then Iseult was living ; then was the tournament ;
then I longed, feared, fought, was angry.
Now if still I fight, fear, am angry,
I know those terminable paths are only paths.

Loneliest of lords, Dinadan smiled ; I feared.
Now no sound is near but aerial screams,
no soft voices, nothing except the harsh
scream of the eagle approaching the plateau of Netzach :

its scream and its passage approaching its primal station
backwards ; about me a scintillation of points,
points of the eagle's plumes, plumes that are paths ;
paths and plumes swoop to the unbelieved symbol.

I left the Prophet ; I lost Iseult ; I failed
to catch the beast out of Broceliande ;
Lancelot forgave me ; if I was christened in that pardon
it was half because I was a greater fool so.

I have gone back, down the road of Logres, the arm
of Iseult, the pass of Monsalvat, into the hut ;
I sit with the old men, as they were ; we sing :
The Lord created all things by means of his Blessing.

I utter the formula ; the formula is all that lives :
sharply the Prophet, Iseult, Lancelot, Dinadan,
call to me this at my dying, and I to them :
The Lord created all things by means of his Blessing.

If this is the kingdom, the power, the glory, my heart
formally offers the kingdom, endures the power,
joins to itself the aerial scream of the eagle . . .
That Thou only canst be Thou only art.

Percivale at Carbonek

In the rent saffron sun hovered the Grail.
Galahad stood in the arch of Carbonek;
the people of Pelles ran to meet him.
  His eyes were sad; he sighed for Lancelot's pardon.

Joy remembered joylessness; joy kneeled
under the arch where Lancelot ran in frenzy.
The astonished angels of the spirit heard him moan:
  Pardon, lord; pardon and bless me, father.

Doubtfully stood the celestial myrmidons, scions
of unremitted beauty; bright feet paused.
Aching with the fibrous infelicity of time,
  pierced his implacability, Galahad kneeled.

The passage through Carbonek was short to the house of
    the Grail;
the wounded king waited for health; motionless
the subdued glory implored the kingdom
  to pardon its power and the double misery of Logres.

Under the arch the Merciful Child
wept for the grief of his father in reconciliation;
who was betrayed there by Merlin and Brisen
  to truth; he saw not; he was false to Guinevere.

Between the Infant and Bors and myself on each hand
under the arch I heard the padding of paws,
woven between us, and the faint howl of the wolf.
   The High Prince shivered in the cold of bleak conjunction.

His hand shook ; pale were his cheeks ;
his head the head of a skull, flesh
cleaving to bone ; his dry voice rattled ;
   ' Pardon, Lord Lancelot ; pardon and blessing, father.'

He knelt silent among the circles of the wolf.
Until the lover of Guinevere acknowledged his son
a bitter frost crept in the bones of Galahad.
   The Host in the Lateran lay in a hid sepulchre.

Stiffly the Child's head turned ; the drawn engine
slewed to his left, to Bors the kin of Lancelot.
He said ' Cousin, can you bear pardon
   to the house of Carbonek from the fallen house of Camelot ? '

Bors answered : ' What should we forgive ? '
' Forgive Us,' the High Prince said, ' for Our existence ;
forgive the means of grace and the hope of glory.
   In the name of Our father forgive Our mother for Our
     birth.'

' Sir,' Bors said, ' only God forgives.
My lord Sir Lancelot my cousin is a lover and kind.
I assent to all, as I pray that my children assent
   and through God join with me in bidding their birth.'

The Infant said : ' Go, cousin.' Bors
stepped from the arch ; the angelic household met him.
The High Prince stepped in his footprints ; into the sun
  Galahad followed Bors ; Carbonek. was entered.

The Last Voyage

The hollow of Jerusalem was a ship.

In the hall of Empire, on the right wall from the stair,
Solomon was painted, a small city and temple
rose beyond, reaching the level of his knee ;
all on a deck floated in a sea of dolphins.
His right hand, blessing, whelmed the djinn
who sank impotently around and drowned in the waters.
Rigid his left arm stretched to the queen Balkis ;
where her mouth on his hand tasted effectual magic,
intellectual art arm-fasted to the sensuous.
Solomon was the grand master of all creaturely being
in sublime necromancy, the rule and road of seeing
for those who have no necessity of existence in themselves ;
On the opposite wall, in a laureate ceremony,
Virgil to Taliessin stretched a shoot
of hazel—the hexameter, the decasyllabic line—
fetched from Homer beyond him ; by the king's poet
were the poets of Logres, Britain, and the ninefold isles :
the isles floated beyond them in a sea of dolphins.
But the actual ship, the hollow of Jerusalem,
beyond the shapes of empire, the capes of Carbonek,
over the topless waves of trenched Broceliande,
drenched by the everlasting spray of existence,
with no mind's sail reefed or set, no slaves at the motived oars,
drove into and clove the wind from unseen shores.
Swept from all altars, swallowed in a path of power

by the wrath that wrecks the pirates in the Narrow Seas,
now in the confidence of the charge, the thrust of the trust,
seizing the sea-curve, the shortest way between points,
to the point of accumulated distance, the safe tension
in each allotted joint of the knotted web of empire,
multiple without dimension, indivisible without uniformity,
the ship of Solomon (blessed be he) drove on.

Fierce in the prow the alchemical Infant burned,
red by celerity now conceiving the white ;
behind him the folded silver column of Percivale,
hands on the royal shoulders, closed wings of flight,
inhaled the fine air of philosophical amazement ;
Bors, mailed in black, completing the trine,
their action in Logres, kneeling on the deck to their right,
the flesh of fatherhood, unique as they in the Will,
prayed still for the need and the bliss of his household.
By three ways of exchange the City sped to the City ;
against the off-shore wind that blew from Sarras
the ship and the song flew.

An infinite flight of doves from the storming sky
of Logres—strangely sea-travellers when the land melts—
forming to overfeather and overwhelm the helm,
numerous as men in the empire, the empire riding
the skies of the ocean, guiding by modulated stresses
on each spoke of the helm the vessel from the realm of Arthur,
lifted oak and elm to a new-ghosted power.
The hosted wings trapped the Infant's song ;
blown back, tossed down, thrown
along the keel, the song hastening the keel

along the curve of the sea-way, the helm fastening
the whole ship to the right balance of the stresses ;
as the fine fair arm of pine-changed Cymodocea,
striking from the grey-green waters of tossed Tiber,
thrust the worshipful duke to the rescue of Rome ;
as the arm of the queen, finger-latched to Solomon's,
matched power to purpose and passion to peace.
The wonder that snapped once in the hollow of Jerusalem
was retrieved now along the level of the bulwark
to where the hands of Galahad were reeved on the prow :
the hollow of Jerusalem was within the hollow of his
          shoulders,
the ban and blessing of the empire ran in his arms,
from his feet the deck spread that was fleet on the sea.
The ship of Solomon (blessed be he) drove on.

Before the helm the ascending-descending sun
lay in quadrilateral covers of a saffron pall
over the bier and the pale body of Blanchefleur,
mother of the nature of lovers, creature of exchange ;
drained there of blood by the thighed wound,
she died another's death, another lived her life.
Where it was still to-night, in the last candles of Logres,
a lady danced, to please the sight of her friends ;
her cheeks were stained from the arteries of Percivale's
          sister.
Between them they trod the measure of heaven and earth,
and the dead woman waited the turn and throe of the dance
where, rafting and undershafting the quadruplicate sacrum,
below the saffron pall, the joyous woe of Blanchefleur,
the ship of Solomon (blessed be he) drove on.

Dinadan was lord of something more than irony,
he died in the deep schismatic war, when Gawaine
hewed the Table in twain, by a feud with his fellows
making peace with his doctrine : he pursued Lancelot
for the Throne's honour, by a side-path with his own.
His brother Agravaine caught the king's dolphin
on the sea-shore, in a track of the bewildered wood,
when by an ambush Lamorack was shot in the back
by the sons of the queen Morgause who slew their mother,
to clean their honour's claws in the earth of her body.
They drew Dinadan to broil on a bed of coals ;
their souls were glad to destroy the pertinence of curiosity ;
the merciful heaven drove the thick smoke to choke him.
But the Infant's song was thick with a litany of names
from the king and the king's friend to the least of the slaves.
He was borne through the waves to his end on a cry of
     substitution.
When he uttered Agravaine's name a light low
covered with flame the spread saffron veil ;
the heart of the dead Dinadan burned on the sun,
and gathered and fled through the air to the head of Percivale,
flew and flamed and flushed the argentine column.
The ship of Solomon (blessed be he) drove on.

Through the sea of omnipotent fact rushed the act of Galahad.
He glowed white ; he leaned against the wind
down the curved road among the topless waters.
He sang *Judica te, Deus* ; the wind,
driven by doves' wings along the arm-taut keel,
sang against itself *Judica te, Deus.*
Prayer and irony had said their say and ceased ;

the sole speech was speed.
In the hollow of Jerusalem the quadrilateral of the sun
was done on the deck beyond Broceliande.
In the monstrum of triangular speed,
in a path of lineal necessity,
the necessity of being was communicated to the son of
    Lancelot.
The ship and the song drove on.

In Logres the King's friend landed, Lancelot of Gaul.
Taliessin at Canterbury met him with the news
of Arthur's death and the overthrow of Mordred.
At the hour of the healing of Pelles
the two kings were one, by exchange of death and healing.
Logres was withdrawn to Carbonek ; it became Britain.

Taliessin at Lancelot's Mass

I came to his altar when dew was bright on the grass;
he—he was not sworn of the priesthood—began the Mass.
The altar was an ancient stone laid upon stones;
Carbonek's arch, Camelot's wall, frame of Bors' bones.

In armour before the earthen footpace he stood;
on his surcoat the lions of his house, dappled with blood,
rampant, regardant; but he wore no helm or sword,
and his hands were bare as Lateran's to the work of our Lord.

In the ritual before the altar Lancelot began to pass;
all the dead lords of the Table were drawn from their graves
    to the Mass;
they stood, inward turned, as shields on a white rushing deck,
between Nimue of Broceliande and Helayne of Carbonek.

In Blanchefleur's cell at Almesbury the queen Guinevere
felt the past exposed; and the detail, sharp and dear,
draw at the pang in the breast till, rich and reconciled,
the mystical milk rose in the mother of Logres' child.

Out of the queen's substitution the wounded and dead king
entered into salvation to serve the holy Thing;
singly seen in the Mass, owning the double Crown,
going to the altar Pelles, and Arthur moving down.

Lancelot and Arthur wove the web ; the sky
opened on moon and sun ; between them, light-traced on
  high,
the unseen knight of terror stood as a friend ;
invisible things and visible waited the end.

Lancelot came to the Canon ; my household stood
around me, bearers of the banners, bounteous in blood ;
each at the earthen footpace ordained to be blessed and to
  bless,
each than I and than all lordlier and less.

Then at the altar We sang in Our office the cycle of names
of their great attributed virtues ; the festival of flames
fell from new sky to new earth ; the light in bands
of bitter glory renewed the imperial lands.

Then the Byzantine ritual, the Epiclesis, began ;
then their voices in Ours invoked the making of man ;
petal on petal floated out of the blossom of the Host,
and all ways the Theotokos conceived by the Holy Ghost.

We exposed, We exalted the Unity ; prismed shone
web, paths, points ; as it was done
the antipodean zones were retrieved round a white rushing
  deck,
and the Acts of the Emperor took zenith from Caucasia to
  Carbonek.

Over the altar, flame of anatomized fire,
the High Prince stood, gyre in burning gyre ;
day level before him, night massed behind ;
the Table ascended ; the glories intertwined.

The Table ascended ; each in turn lordliest and least—
slave and squire, woman and wizard, poet and priest ;
interchanged adoration, interdispersed prayer,
the ruddy pillar of the Infant was the passage of the porphyry
     stair.

That which had been Taliessin rose in the rood ;
in the house of Galahad over the altar he stood,
manacled by the web, in the web made free ;
there was no capable song for the joy in me :

joy to new joy piercing from paths foregone ;
that which had been Taliessin made joy to a Joy unknown ;
manifest Joy speeding in a Joy unmanifest.
Lancelot's voice below sang : *Ite ; missa est.*

Fast to the Byzantine harbour gather the salvaged sails ;
that which was once Taliessin rides to the barrows of Wales
up the vales of the Wye ; if skill be of work or of will
in the dispersed homes of the household, let the Company
     pray for it still.

NOTE

These references are not intended to help the poems as poems. All that comes from Malory is, I think, familiar, but though he provided many hints in his images he does not seem to trouble to work out the possibilities of relation. I have summarized a few as they are used here, and made what other acknowledgements are due.

Title.] This was not taken from Tennyson, but it was confirmed later by a line in *The Holy Grail* :

Taliessin is our fullest throat of song.

pp. 3 and 4.] The images in the third and fourth stanzas are those used of a particular state of being in *Comus*, the *Nightingale Ode*, the *Prelude*, and the *Divine Comedy*.

pp. 15 et seq.] Bors was the nephew of Lancelot, and the companion of Galahad and Percivale. He had two children by Elayne, the daughter of King Brangoris, ' and sauf for her syre Bors was a clene mayden '.

pp. 20 et seq.] Lamorack was the brother of Percivale and Blanchefleur. He was the lover of the queen Morgause of Orkney, Arthur's sister. The two were killed by her sons, Gawaine and Agravaine, for the honour of the house of Orkney.

pp. 39–41.] After the dolorous blow struck against King Pelles in Carbonek by Balin the Savage, Balin and Balan his brother killed each other unknowingly, and Arthur unknowingly committed incest with his sister Morgause, who became by him the mother of Mordred.

p. 45.] The quotation from Heracleitus was taken from Mr. Yeats's book, *A Vision*.

p. 56.] ' the feeling intellect' is from the *Prelude*, Book 14.

p. 69.] Galahad came to Caerleon after Palomides had been christened on the Feast of Pentecost. ' In the honour of the hyghness of Galahad he was ledde in to kinge Arthurs chamber and there rested in his own bedde '—*Morte d'Arthur*, Book XIII. The image of the stone and shell is from the *Prelude*, Book 5.

p. 75.] The variation of the Merlin tale is due to Swinburne (but this Merlin is young): *Tristram of Lyonesse*, Books 1 and 6.

p. 78.] Netzach is a station on the Sephirotic Tree; its quality is Victory.

p. 86.] Blanchefleur died from a letting of blood to heal a sick lady; her body was taken by the three lords of the quest, and buried 'in the spyrytual place'.

p. 90.] 'the unseen knight' was Garlon, the brother of King Pelles. It was through the quarrel with him that Balin the Savage came to strike the dolorous blow at Pelles 'with the same spere that Longeus smote oure lord to the hearte', so that 'he myght never be hole tyl Galahad the haute prince heled him in the quest of the Sangraille.'

THE REGION OF THE SUMMER STARS

by CHARLES WILLIAMS

Contents

Preface

THESE poems are part of a series of poems which began with *Taliessin through Logres*, but these, generally, are incidental to the main theme.

That theme is what was anciently called the Matter of Britain; that is, the reign of King Arthur in Logres and the Achievement of the Grail. Logres is Britain regarded as a province of the Empire with its centre at Byzantium. The time historically is after the conversion of the Empire to Christianity but during the expectation of the Return of Our Lord (the Parousia). The Emperor of the poem, however, is to be regarded rather as operative Providence. On the south-western side of Logres lies the region of Broceliande, in which is Carbonek where the Grail and other Hallows are in the keeping of King Pelles and his daughter Helayne. Beyond the seas of Broceliande is the holy state of Sarras. In the antipodean seas is the opposite and infernal state of P'o-l'u.

Nothing more is, I think, necessary to these poems. But in general the argument of the series is the expectation of the return of Our Lord by means of the Grail and of the establishment of the kingdom of Logres (or Britain) to this end by the powers of the Empire and Broceliande. Logres, however, was distracted by its own sins, and the wounding of King Pelles (the Keeper of the Hallows) by the Lord Balin the Savage was the Dolorous Blow which prevented the union of Carbonek and Logres and therefore the coming of the Grail. There followed, by a heavenly substitution, the begetting of Galahad by Lancelot on the Princess Helayne in an enchantment. Galahad is brought up in a Convent of White Nuns under the care of Dindrane, Percivale's sister. Afterwards he goes to the court of Arthur and then departs, together with Percivale and Bors, for Carbonek and Sarras where he finally achieves the Grail. Meanwhile wars break out between Arthur and Lancelot through which, and through the treachery of Mordred the King's bastard son, Logres is overthrown and afterwards becomes the historical Britain, in which the myth of its origin remains.

1944   C. W.

Prelude

IRONY was the Fortune of Athens; Rome came
to pluck the Fortune of Athens, and stand embattled
as in arms, so in mind against evil luck.
A few wise masters devised for the heart
a road from the universe into dematerialized spirit,
but most prattled cunning preventive doctrine;
till on a day from a hill in the middle of Athens
where men adored Irony the unknown lord,
Paul sent over Athens and Rome his call:
'Whom ye ignorantly worship, him I declare.'

The crooked smiles of the Greeks
fled from their faces while thorned-in-the-flesh the Apostle
against their defensive inflections of verb and voice,
their accents of presaged frustration, their sterile protections,
named in its twyfold Nature the golden Ambiguity.
Then for the creature he invented the vocabulary of faith;
he defined in speech the physiological glory
and began to teach the terms of the work of glory.
The young Church breakfasted on glory; handfasted,
her elect functioned in the light. But the ancient intellect
heard, delaying and playing with its archives, and demurred
that pain was easy, and completeness of belief costly,
and flesh too queasy to bear the main of spirit.

The converted doctors turned to their former confessions,
the limitary heresiarchs feared the indiscretions of matter,
and the careful Nestorius, coming to befriend peace,
preached in Byzantium. Before the sermon was at end
the metaphysicians, sitting to note him, heard
from the City the roar of burning and bundled torches
rise through the fixed stars: *Theotokos, Anthropotokos;*
his disciples shrank from the blood-stream where the full torches
ruddily poured round the eikon of Mary-in-blessing.
Professing only a moral union, they fled
from the new-spread bounty; they found a quarrel with the Empire
and the sustenance of Empire, with the ground of faith and earth,
the golden and rose-creamed flesh of the grand Ambiguity.

Fast as they, the orthodox imagination
seized on the Roman polity; there, for a day,
beyond history, holding history at bay,
it established through the themes of the Empire the condition of
     Christendom
and saw everywhere manumission of grace into glory.
Beyond the ancient line of imperial shapes
it saw the Throne of primal order, the zone
of visionary powers, and almost (in a cloud) the face
of the only sublime Emperor; as John once
in Patmos, so then all the Empire in Byzantium:
the Acts of the Throne were borne by the speeding logothetes,
and the earth flourished, hazel, corn, and vine.

The Empire, in the peace of the Emperor,
expected perfection; it awaited the Second Coming

of the Union, of the twy-natured single Person,
centuries-belated, now to be; but how
only a few saints knew, in Apennine
or Egypt or Cappadocia, monk or nun,
slave or princess or poet, or, white in Lateran,
like the ghost of man awaiting his body, the Pope.
Hope, as by night the first of the summer stars
in the universal sky high hung,
in them looked on the sea, and across the sea
saw coming, from the world of the Three-in-One,
in a rich container, the Blood of the Deivirilis,
communicated everywhere, but there singly borne,
and the morn of the Trinity rising through the sea to the sun.

The Empire lay in the imposed order; around
the Throne the visionary zone of clear light
hummed with celestial action; there the forms
of chamberlains, logothetes, nuncios, went and came,
diagrams of light moving in the light; they lacked
the flesh and blood, the golden cream and the rose
tinctures; these dwelled in Byzantium; they were held
in men and women, or even (as named qualities)
in the golden day and the rose-gardens of Caucasia.
But also in the mind of the Empire another kind
of tale lay than that of the Grail; those
who worked in the ports heard shipmen say
that in the antipodean ocean was a sight
known only to the Emperor's lordliest admirals
who, closeliest obeying command, passed
near to the harbour and vile marshes of P'o-l'u;

there on the waves a headless Emperor walked
coped in a foul indecent crimson; octopods
round him stretched giant tentacles and crawled
heavily on the slimy surface of the tangled sea,
goggling with lidless eyes at the coast of the Empire.

This, fable or truth, none knew
except the high sea-lords; enough
that in the stuff of the Empire the quality of irony
flickered and faded before the capacity of faith;
all the peoples awaited the Parousia, all
the themes vibrated with duty and expectation
of the coming of the vessel where, ere the Deposition,
the blood of the golden single-personed Ambiguity
fulfilled its commission and was caught; then for a season
was hidden in its own place, till at last (bidden
by ultimate Reason) it deigned at last emerge
out of the extreme verge of the west and the east;
priest and victim. Only the women of earth,
by primal dispensation, little by themselves understood,
shared with that Sacrifice the victimization of blood.

The Calling of Taliessin

BY some it was said that Taliessin
was a child of Henwg the saint, bred in Caerleon,
and thence come, miracle-commissioned; by some
that he sprang from the bards, the ancient guards of the cauldron
called of Ceridwen; she goddess or priestess,
Tydeg Voel's wife, whose life was legend,
and he if her son then so by magic: none
knew; no clue he showed when he rode down the Wye
coracle-cradled, and at the weir was seen
by Elphin the son of Gwyddno and drawn to shore.
The men with Elphin then could only stare
at the bright forehead of the lonely river-fugitive,
the child coming from the wild Druid wood.
Could they believe in the light that lived from his brow?
decision, there as here, was the mind's election,
the arbitration of faith, the erection of the City.
But Elphin was a man of the tribes, his vocation the blood's,
nor could feel, in more than a chorus after a meal,
verse; vainly Taliessin's first song
through river-mated rhythms while he smiled at the sky
pulsated; only in the song a recurrent code
showed the child already initiated
in the changes of the cauldron of Ceridwen, from the fish to the
　　frog,

from the frog to the crow, from the crow to the leaping roe,
from the roe to the kindled fire, from fire to wheat,
from the wheat to the cooked loaf, from shapes that eat
to shapes that are eaten, and then to the fish split
to be at once on the dish and again in the sea—
the fated cycle communicated in heathen secrets;
for the Lord God had not yet set him at liberty,
nor shown him the doctrine of largesse in the land of the Trinity.

In Elphin's house he grew and practised verse;
striving in his young body with the double living
of the breath in the lung and the sung breath in the brain,
the growing and the knowing and the union of both in the show-
 ing,
the triune union in each line of verse,
but lacking the formulæ and the grand backing of the Empire.
Yet then his heart, ears, and eyes were wise
from Druid secrets in the twilight and the sun-dawn;
his hearing caught each smallest singular cry
of bird and beast; almost he talked their talk;
his sight followed each farthest flight, each small
insect-dance-pattern in the air; he knew
correspondence and the law of similitudes; he had seen the caul-
 dron
of poetry and plenty; he heard now dimly
of the food that freed from the cycle, of the butteries of the monks
and the baps and beans of hermits in Thule and the Thebaid.
When Elphin asked him his lineage, he sang riddling:
'My heritage is all men's; only my age is my own.
I am a wonder whose origin is not known.

I carried in battle a banner before Lleon of Lochlin,
and held in the sleeping-chamber a mirror for his queen.
I am more than the visions of all men and my own vision,
and my true region is the summer stars.
I suffered in dreams derision for the son of a virgin,
yet I stood in the Galaxy at the throne of the Distributor
and flew over the waves when the world was in flood.
I rose to the third heaven with her of the penitence
and was tangled through every sense by the hazel bush;
I was mangled for a night and a day by black swine,
yet my true region is the summer stars.
I was thrall to Ceridwen and free in the manger of an ass.
Before speech came to pass, I was full of the danger of loquacity.
It is a doubt if my body is flesh or fish,
therefore no woman will ever wish to bed me
and no man make true love without me.
All the doctors come to stand about me,
yet I shall never have any near me to need me.
Every king shall call me Taliessin,
and till the doom I am handfast with all the dead.'

Before Wye from his father Henwg, or else
from a wandering priest among the vales of Wye
Taliessin heard a word of the Empire; he heard
tales of the tree of Adam, and the rare superfluity
of moral creation, till the will of the superfluity
turned the tree to a rood for itself and Another
and envenomed its blood with mood; then the will of its Origin
shared the blood and fared forth well from the tree.
Dim and far came the myth to Taliessin

over the dark rim of the southern sea.
Poor, goetic or theurgic, the former spells
seemed beside the promise of greater formulæ;
poor—control or compact—the personal mastery,
the act of magic, or the strain of ancient verse
beside the thickening dreams of the impersonal Empire
and the moulded themes of the Empire; and they all
from Gaul to Jerusalem enfolded in the infinite hall
of the Sacred Emperor at operative Byzantium.
His heart turned to know more than could be learned
by Wye of that white healing metaphysic;
he sought the sea and the City; he was caught by a rumour.

On his shoulder a covered harp, and he cloaked
over his tunic; laced boots of hide
on his feet, and a sword of Rome slung by his side,
he turned to the towns of the coast; shipping had failed,
yet sometimes a vessel sailed to the ports of Gaul
from the southern edge of the Isle of the Sea; there
he looked to find passage and then to forage
in holy luck—by singing verses, by writing
letters or carrying, by script-copying or fighting,—
nay, if need were, by currying horses
for the dukes of the Empire whose courses took them to By-
    zantium.
As he came on the third day down the way to the coast
he saw on his left a wilderness; Logres lay
without the form of a Republic, without letters or law,
a storm of violent kings at war—smoke
poured from a burning village in the mid-east;

transport had ceased, and all exchange stilled.
On the other hand was the wood of Broceliande.

Dangerous to men is the wood of Broceliande.
Hardly the Druid, hardly a Christian priest,
pierced it ever; it was held, then as now,
by those few who in Britain study the matter of the marches
that there the divine science and the grand art,
if at all below the third heaven, know
their correspondence, and live in a new style—
many a mile of distance goes to the making:
but those fewer, now as then, who enter
come rarely again with brain unravished
by the power of the place—some by grace dumb
and living, like a blest child, in a mild and holy
sympathy of joy; but the rest loquacious with a graph
or a gospel, gustily audacious over three heavens.

Between the anarchy of yet unmade Logres
and the darkness of secret-swayed Broceliande
Taliessin took his way; his way curved
on that stormy day so near the wood that he saw
a dark rose of sunset between tree and tree
lie on the sea, the antipodean ocean
beheld there in thrusting inlets; his heart
beat lest dread or desolation wrecked his mind
so that he fell from his kind, and the grand art failed—
control lost and all sense crossed;
or else he quit no more for a thrilling rhyme,
fulfilling a time of attention, but O pledged

beyond himself to an edged anguish dividing
word from thing and uniting thing to word—
each guiding and each fighting the other.
'It is a doubt if my body is flesh or fish,'
he sang in his grief; 'hapless the woman who loves me,
hapless I—flung alive where only
the cold-lipped mermen thrive among staring creatures
of undersea, or lost where the beast-natures
in a wood of suicides lap at the loss of intellect.'
Obscurely his future—the king's poet's future—
shook in his blood; his look was held by the flood
angrily rose-darkened down the inlets of the wood.

He forced his eyes again to the road; far
before him, on to the road from the wood's mass,
he saw a form pass; it hovered and turned
towards him along the road, as if to challenge,
check, or wreck his journey. The sun had sunk,
the rose vanished from the under-sea—and he
banished there between Logres and Broceliande
to feel before him the road threaten ravage
and the power of universal spirit rise
against him to be wild and savage on his lonely spirit;
all things combined, and defined themselves in that moment
hostile to him and the burning homes of Logres.
He saw draw towards him a faint light
clearer and sharper than sun or moon; nearer
as it drew it grew double; his hand found
his sword, his heart sang an invocation
of the woman whose name he had heard in a tale of the myth,

of Mary Magdalene who had charity for Christ—she
to him in his grief as he to her in her sin.
Bright-keen at first, the light grew soft;
the double aureole was entwining a double shape,
gently-shining—as in the days to be
the king's poet himself at the court of Camelot
might seem (could his heart have guessed) to his true lovers.
The double shape divided to a man and a woman,
pricking his eyes with the quiet shining of their skin,
tall, slender, black-haired; they spared a width
between themselves and him, coming to a pause,
and he also, prepared for any chance.

Time and space, duration and extension, to a child
are in the father's voice, the mother's face,
and to us in things passing or pausing in passing,
amassing themselves in that pause to a new energy
for or against the soul's motion; Taliessin
felt before him an accumulation of power
tower in the two shapes, so deep in calm
that it seemed the word of the heart and the word of the voice
must find, in each and in both, correspondence there
more than even the grand art could know or show
for all similitudes; he heard speech flow
out of the masculine mouth of the twinned form
as the south wind, stirring the tiny waves, shows
and shakes the stillness of the wide accumulated air.
'Whither, Taliessin—whither, son of the bards—
moves the song that blows you along our marches?'
Taliessin said: 'Who asks?' and the other: 'Merlin

am I; she Brisen my sister; we are free
of the forest, parthenogenetical in Broceliande
from the Nature, from Nimue our mother; sent are we
to build, as is willed, Logres, and in Logres a throne
like that other of Carbonek, of King Pelles in Broceliande,
the holder of the Hallows; my sister shall stand in his house
to tend his daughter in the day of her destiny, but I
make haste to Logres, to call and install King Arthur;
at whose board you and I, lord, again may meet.'
Taliessin said: 'Are you mortal? are you a friend?
I do not know Arthur; I go from Wye
to find beyond sea a fact or a fable.'
Merlin answered: 'A friend, mortal or immortal,
if you choose; we bear no arms; and for harms spiritual
we two can placably receive the Names spoken
in Byzantium, which shall be by Thames; it is ordered that soon
the Empire and Broceliande shall meet in Logres,
and the Hallows be borne from Carbonek into the sun.
Therefore Nimue our mother directs in Carbonek
the maidenhood of Pelles' daughter Helayne, and I
go to prepare Logres for the sea-coming
from Sarras.' Taliessin said: 'Where is Sarras?'
But Merlin: 'Hush; formulæ and rhymes are yours
but seek no more; fortunate the poet who endures
to measure in his mind the distance even to Carbonek;
few dare more—enough. The Peace be with you.'
Taliessin gazed at the twins and his heart was stilled;
he said: 'And with you be the Peace.' Then Brisen: 'Sleep
we three here to-night and wait for the day.'

Done was the day; the antipodean sun
cast earth's coned shadow into space;
it exposed the summer stars; as they rose
the light of Taliessin's native land
shone in a visible glory over him sleeping.
Rarely through the wood rang a celestial cry,
sometimes with a like reply, sometimes with none.
The trees shook, in no breeze, to a passage of power.
Under the ground was the sound of great waves
breaking round huge caves, ancient sepulchres,
where Ocean, a young child of making, held
talk with the first mother of making, Nimue:—
or so might seem to the dream of the young poet;
or else the noise gave voice to the image in his brain,
an image springing from a tangle of ringing names—
Thames, Camelot, Carbonek, Pelles and Arthur,
Logres, Wye, Helayne, Broceliande,
Byzantium, the Empire . . . the Empire . . . 'this', the voice
sang, 'is the Empire; what serves the Empire?' The youth
was caught by a pulse of truth in the image; he saw
Merlin and Brisen rise from their sleep and kiss.
He saw in the light of the stars above him Merlin
draw near and stoop; he felt the black-haired wizard
breathe on his eyes, saying: 'Do not wake, king's poet.
Fate is for you to find but for us to make.
Dream—or see in dream. The rite opens.
Lie you still to-night, as in vales of Wye.'

The cone's shadow of earth fell into space,
and into (other than space) the third heaven.

In the third heaven are the living unriven truths,
climax tranquil in Venus. Merlin and Brisen
heard, as in faint bee-like humming
round the cone's point, the feeling intellect hasten
to fasten on the earth's image; in the third heaven
the stones of the waste glimmered like summer stars.
Between wood and waste the yoked children of Nimue
opened the rite; they invoked the third heaven,
heard in the far humming of the spiritual intellect,
to the building of Logres and the coming of the land of the Trinity
which is called Sarras in maps of the soul. Merlin
made preparation; on the ground he drew the pentagram,
at four corners he dropped the sacred herbs,
sharp odours; under his hands they became
flame of potential intellect becoming actual,
allaying the mortal air with purification.
At the fifth angle, naked in the hypnotic trance,
hands caught behind her at the base of sense
as at the centre of space, Brisen stood,
the impassioned diagram of space; her shadow fell
east into Logres, cast by the fourfold fire.
The abstract gaze of Merlin overlooked
his sister, as time space; the elementals became
the magical continuum, where Merlin saw the place
to prepare, and himself to fare to the preparation.
He lifted the five times cross-incised rod
and began incantation; in the tongue of Broceliande
adjuring all the primal atoms of earth
to shape the borders of Logres, to the dispensation
of Carbonek to Caerleon, of Caerleon to Camelot, to the union

of King Pelles and King Arthur, to the sea-coming of Sarras
which beneath the Throne is shown in mosaics to Byzantium.

The weight of poetry could not then sink
into the full depth of the weight of glory.
For all the codes his young tongue bore
Taliessin could not think in Merlin's style,
nor his verse grow mature with pure fact.
Many a mile of distance in the Empire was to go
to the learning, many a turn of exchange in the need
of himself or others or the Empire, much speed
in chariots and ships by the Golden Horn, and the high
cliffs and gardens of Caucasus, and the sky of Rome
where the hands of the Pope are precise in the white sacrifice.
The operation of Merlin passed through his sleep
by accidents, not by events; nor could his heart
elect and effect the full purpose of formulæ.
But the accidents hinted the events. He saw the pillared
back of Brisen ruddy in the fires' glow,
and the fires' glow reddening the snow of mountains
where his track ran—no more a back, but himself
climbing from meadow-grasses to the rough passes
of frosty heights, crossing Apennine, or tossing
under forked lightning on Caspian below Caucasus.
Everywhere his road ran ranging the themes,
and near a clear city on a sea-site
in a light that shone from behind the sun; the sun
was not so fierce as to pierce where that light could
through every waste and wood; the city and the light
lay beyond the sun and beyond his dream,

nor could the weight of poetry sink so far
as the weight of glory; on the brink of the last depth
the glory clouded to its own covering and became
again the recapitulatory body of Brisen,
the engine of the First Mover, fit to his wit
that works in earth the birth of superfluous good:
fair let the creature follow that Nature. Taliessin
began then to share in the doctrine of largesse
that should mark in Camelot the lovers of the king's poet;
he saw again the wide waste of Logres
under the dark and mighty shadow of Brisen,
cast by the clear assuaging fires; in the shadow
the stones of the waste glimmered like summer stars;
he heard again the presaging spell of Merlin
foretell and furnish the lofty errand of Logres.

The stars vanished; they gone, the illumined dusk
under the spell darkened to the colour of porphyry,
the colour of the stair of Empire and the womb of woman,
and the rich largesse of the Emperor; within was a point,
deep beyond or deep within Logres,
as if it had swallowed all the summer stars
and hollowed the porphyry night for its having and holding—
tiny, dark-rose, self-glowing,
as a firefly's egg or (beyond body and spirit,
could the art of the king's poet in the court of Camelot,
after his journeys, find words for body or spirit)
the entire point of the thrice co-inherent Trinity
when every crown and every choir is vanished,
and all sight and hearing is nothing else.

It burned for a moment as short as itself tiny,
and inturned to its disappearing, as the voice of Merlin
sang: 'Go, son of the bards; king's poet,
go; propolitan are the porphyry chambers; see
and know the Empire; fulfil then an errand;
rescue the king at Mount Badon; stand by the king,
Arthur, the king we make, until the land
of the Trinity by a sea-coming fetch to his stair.
Sarras is free to Carbonek, Carbonek to Camelot;
in all categories holds the largesse of exchange,
and the sea of Broceliande enfolds the Empire.'

The shadow of Brisen lay on the whole of Logres,
but the shadow was a flight of dark stairs, from the brain
to the base; the pavement of the base, below all,
lay in the trees and seas of Broceliande.
But in the visionary sleep, at the height of the flight,
where the brain of Logres opened in the main of space,
grew a golden throne, of two dragons twined,
where a king sat crowned, around him figures
of great lords; Taliessin saw himself
stand on the king's left hand among the lords.
His own voice had just sung and ceased.
All were gazing, and he, near the king's chair,
down the stair; they waited and watched for a coming,
for the sea-coming of the Trinity through Broceliande.
So full were they fixed that his sleeping eyes pricked
to see and feel their gaze; at once, with the pricking
he swung to the waves on the deck of a moving ship,
drawing to the watchers: but whether the king's poet's style

and desire for verse palpitated in the young Taliessin
to more than his function, and rated himself in sleep
higher than any crude folly, waking, could;
or whether Brisen and the operation of the rite
wrought in his brain to an emanation of Nimue,
the mother of all operation; or whether some true
foreboding grew of Dindrane the sister of Percivale,
she who was called Blanchfleur in religion, and to be
farther from and closer to the king's poet
than any, the eidolon of his beatitude, his blood's bounty;
or whether Merlin among all the phantasmagoria
showed him the final term and the firm purpose
of heaven, and the errand of Helayne the daughter of Pelles
—there, on the deck above the flood, stood
the daughter of a king, holding an unseen thing
between her hands, but over her hands a veil,
the saffron veil of the sun itself, covered
all; her face was pale with stress of passion
as the ship ran—and even in a sleep within a sleep
Taliessin trembled; terrible was the form of the princess,
the covered shape terrible; as the stupor loosed
he saw himself below himself asleep
deep within the protective pentagram, where burned
the four fires, and Brisen self-fiery,
at the five angles, and the tree-tangles beyond
in the first beginning, in the spinning of Merlin's spells
when the wise twins came from the wood: but all that stood
at the height of the brain faded into the space
again of a starry night; through the reach of Logres
the stones of the waste glimmered like summer stars,

as if the king's poet's household of stars
shone, in a visible glory, on the dreaming Taliessin.
The spells of Merlin worked in each episode of time,
each code of initiation, each vocation and rule,
each school of power, the foundation of Camelot, the bond
of the two kings in Carbonek, Caerleon, and Camelot,
of the Holder of the Hallows and the new-designed house
of the Hallows in the Empire. Taliessin's brain lost
again the vision of Imagination at the full;
he heard the final voice of Merlin lull
once more his body and mind to deep sleep:
'Son of the bards, go; go, Taliessin;
take the track of the Empire; go to Byzantium.
Thereafter you shall buy souls in many markets,
low be the purchase or high—all's low,
so the show of summer stars be thereby heightened.
If in the end anything fail of all
purposed by our mother and the Emperor, if the term
be held less firm in Camelot than in Carbonek,
as well my sister and I may guess now
and prepare the ambiguous rite for either chance
in the kingdom of Arthur; if cease the coming from the seas
at the evil luck of a blow dolorously struck,
it may be that this gathering of souls, that the king's poet's household
shall follow in Logres and Britain the spiritual roads
that the son of Helayne shall trace westward through the trees
of Broceliande; they who shall be called and thralled
by Taliessin's purchase and their own will
from many a suburb, many a waste; say

that they are a wonder whose origin is not known,
they are strown with a high habit, with the doctrine of largesse,
who in his house shall be more than the king's poet
because of the vows they take; but now haste
all we three on the roads—Brisen to Carbonek,
I to Camelot, and Taliessin to Byzantium.'

In the morning, they rose, ate, blessed each other,
bade farewell, and parted—Brisen to Carbonek,
Merlin to Camelot, and Taliessin to Byzantium.

Taliessin in the Rose-Garden

THE king's poet walked among the queen's roses
　(all kinds all minds taking),
making verse, putting distance into verse,
cutting and trimming verse as the gardeners the roses.
He turned, at a path's end, between two bushes
of cabbage-roses, scions of Caucasia, *centifoliæ*,
hearts folded strong in a hundred meanings.
Along the level spinal path Taliessin,
his eyes abused by the crimson, confused saw
for a moment in the middle distance a rush of the crimson
shaping at the garden's entrance to a triple form,
to three implicit figures of the mind; his eyes
cleared; appeared three women of Camelot—
the feminine headship of Logres, the queen Guinevere,
talking to Dindrane, Percivale's sister; beyond,
as the ground-work she was and tended, a single maid
hardened with toil on the well-gardened roses:
what was even Dindrane but an eidolon of the slaves?

The air was clear, as near as earth can
to the third heaven, climax tranquil in Venus.
Only (what lacks there) it breathed the energy
from Broceliande that ever seethed in Logres,
the variable temperature of mastering Nature; Taliessin's

senses under Nimue's influences stirred and trembled
with the infinite and infinitesimal trembling of the roses.
At the entrance to the long rose-path he saw
the sensuous mode, the consummate earth of Logres,
the wife of Arthur, the queen of the kingdom, Guinevere.
Hazel-lithe she stood, in a green gown;
bare against the green, her arm was tinged
with faint rose-veins, and golden-flecked
as the massed fair hair under the gold
circlet of Logres; on one hand was the ring
of the consort of Logres; deep-rose-royal
it drew the rose-alleys to its magical square.
There, in the single central ruby, Taliessin
saw, in the sovereign gem of Logres, the contained
life of Logres-in-the-Empire; till the flush of the roses
let seem that the unrestrained rush of the ruby
loosed a secular war to expand through the land,
and again the shore of Logres—and that soon—
felt the pirate beaks in a moon of blood-letting;
and within, yet encircling, the war, the sacred stone
shook with the infinitesimal trembling of the roses
and melted inwards into the blood of the king
Pelles, belted by the curse of the Dolorous Blow;
so rich was the ring and by Merlin royally runed.
The path of the garden was a verse into the wound,
into the secrets of Carbonek and the queen's majesty,
in the king's poet's mouth; he heard himself say:
'The Wounded Rose runs with blood at Carbonek.'

Making the poem he made, he heard himself

say in the rose-garden to the queen of Logres—
she? he spoke low; she talked and laughed;
under her brow she looked for the king's friend
Lancelot. Taliessin heard himself say:
'Tristram and Mark were in love with the Queen Iseult.
Palomides studied her more; so I
everywhere study and sigh for the zodiac in flesh—
scandal to men, folly to women! but we,
Palomides and I, see everywhere the hint,
in a queen's shape or a slave's; we bid for a purchase;
the purchase flies to its aim in the heart of another;
our fame is left us darkling, and our mind to find
a new law; bitter is the brew of exchange.
We buy for others; we make beauty for others;
and the beauty made is not the beauty meant:
shent is pride while the Rose-King bleeds at Carbonek.

'Scandal to the pious Jews, folly to the sly Greeks!
But I was Druid-born and Byzantium-trained.
Beyond Wye, by the cauldron of Ceridwen, I saw
the golden sickle flash in the forest, and heard
the pagans mutter a myth; thence by the ocean
dreaming the matter of Logres I came where the hierarchs
patter the sacred names on the golden floor
under the Throne of Empire; I saw how the City
was based, faced fair to the Emperor as the queen to the king,
slaves to lords, and all Caucasia to Carbonek.
The magnanimous stair rose in the hall of Empire.
The Acts of Identity issued from the Throne; there
twelve images were shown in a mystery, twelve

zodiacal houses; the sun of the operative Emperor
wended through them, attended by the spiritual planets,
attributing to the themes their qualities of cause and permanence:
in each the generation of creation, in each the consummation.
All coalesced in each; that each mind
in the Empire might find its own kind of entry.
Aquarius for me opened the principle of eyes
in the clearness above the firmament; I saw below,
patterned in the stellar clearness, the rosed femininity
particled out of the universe, the articled form
of the Eve in the Adam; the Adam known in the Eve.
To visionary eyes the path of man began
to pass through the themes and the houses; can I recall
all? shall even the queen be seen in the full
glory now in Camelot outside Byzantium?
Nay, say only that the Twins ran in the arms
and laired in the hands, in the queen's hands, in Rome
the City of Twins, wolf-twins, cubs
humanized to labour, making muscles and thumbs,
that each might neighbour the other to instruments and events.
The Scorpion-contingency, controlled and ensouled in Jerusalem,
held its privy place; the Acts of Identity
furnished with danger the anger of the laden tail.
Earth and the queen's body had base in Libra.
Glorious over Logres, let the headship of the queen
be seen, as Caucasia to Carbonek, as Logres to Sarras.

'Within and without the way wove about the image,
about the City and the body; I followed the way
from the eyes; it was swallowed in the sweet dark pit

of the palms—lit how? lit by the rays
from the golden-growthed, golden-clothed arms,
golden-sheathed and golden-breathed, imperially
shining from above toward instruments and events,
rays shaken out towards the queen's hand stretched
to welcome the king's friend, or a slave's to trim
the rose or pluck a nut from the uncut hazel,
or the princess Dindrane's to the fair conclusion of prayer.
Under the flashes, down a steep stair, I came
to a deep figure; I came to the house of Libra.
Libra in the category of flesh is the theme of Caucasia,
the mesh of the net of the imperially bottomed glory;
and the frame of justice and balance set in the body,
the balance and poise needful to all joys
and all peace. I studied universal justice
between man and man, and (O opposite!) between man and
    woman
by their own skill and the will of the Throne; light
compact in each fitting act of justice in the City,
and support-in-the-flesh of the sitting body of beauty.
Scandal to the Jews, folly to the Greeks! let the hazel
of verse measure the multifold levels of unity.

Under the rays I studied arch-natural justice.
Suddenly at a moment the rays ranged wild
and the darting light changed. The roseal pattern
'ran together, and was botched and blotched, blood
inflaming the holy dark; the way of return
climbed beside the timed and falling blood.

'The zodiac of Christ poorly sufficed the Adam;
they bade the Scorpion sting; they looked wildly
on the crookt curves of identity; venom is hereditary,
and the Adam's children endure the Adam's blood.
Cain, seeking a cure, was driven farther
into the pit; at a blow he split the zodiac.
He called into being earthly without heavenly justice,
supposing without his brother, without the other,
he solely existed: fool! the rosed shape
vanished; instead, the clearness of Aquarius was bloodshot,
the Twins for very nearness tore each other:
the way climbed against timed and falling blood,
by a secular stair of months, deep-rose-royal.
And I there climbing in the night's distance
till the clear light shone on the height's edge:
out of the pit and the split zodiac I came
to the level above the magnanimous stair, and saw
the Empire dark with the incoherence of the houses.
Nay, there, as I looked on the stretched Empire
I heard, as in a throb of stretched verse,
the women everywhere throughout it sob with the curse
and the altars of Christ everywhere offer the grails.
Well are women warned from serving the altar
who, by the nature of their creature, from Caucasia to Carbonek,
share with the Sacrifice the victimization of blood.
Flesh knows what spirit knows,
but spirit knows it knows—categories of identity:
women's flesh lives the quest of the Grail
in the change from Camelot to Carbonek and from Carbonek
     to Sarras,

puberty to Carbonek, and the stanching, and Carbonek **to**
    death.
Blessed is she who gives herself to the journey.

'Flesh tells what spirit tells
(but spirit knows it tells). Women's travel
holds in the natural the image of the supernatural,
the shed metrical of the shed anthropometrical.
Truth speeds from the taunt, and Pelles bleeds
below Jupiter's red-pierced planet; the taunt
yields to the truth, irony to defeated irony.
The phosphor of Percivale's philosophical star
shines down the roads of Logres and Broceliande;
happy the woman who in the light of Percivale
feels Galahad, the companion of Percivale, rise
in her flesh, and her flesh bright in Carbonek with Christ,
in the turn of her body, in the turn of her flesh, in the turn
of the Heart that heals itself for the healing of others,
the only Heart that healed itself without others,
when our Lord recovered the Scorpion and restored the
    zodiac.
Blessed is she who can know the Dolorous Blow
healed in the flesh of Pelles, the flesh of women;
and hears softly with touched ears in Camelot
Merlin magically prepare for the Rite of Galahad
and the fixing of all fidelity from all infidelity.

'This I saw in a chamber of Byzantium; the princess
Dindrane again opened my eyes in Aquarius.
Let the queen's majesty, the feminine headship of Logres,

deign to exhibit the glory to the women of Logres;
each to one vision, but the queen for all.
Bring to a flash of seeing the women in the world's base.'

Taliessin saw the queen from the Throne, again
from the rose-garden; she talked sideways to Dindrane.
The king's poet came to the entrance; the queen said,
with the little scorn that becomes a queen of Logres:
'Has my lord dallied with poetry among the roses'

The Departure of Dindrane

THE household waited in the court; the day was curst
with a rain that had not abated since first dawn.
Hoods and cloaks covered helms and gowns.
An armed escort was in the van and the rear
more for parade than precaution; little chance
that any pirate should raid the realm's best.
In the centre a few girls talked, and squires
held horses ready for the two lords—
Taliessin riding with Dindrane to the convent at Almesbury.

Logres kept the old Levitical law;
each slave, at the end of seven years,
was freed, in the change of flesh, from the mesh of bondage.
The jubilee came: and he free or she
before the king's bailiff was called to make choice
with his own voice—either to be landed oversea
by a Government ship, crowns in purse, at the nearest
port to his own dearest land: or in Logres
to be given—for a woman a dowry, for a man a farm
or a place in a guild or the army; or, last,
to compact again with a free heart's love
in what household was sweet alike to past and future.

One of the company, a girl bought in Athens,

for some trick of Taliessin's judgement or tenderness, and brought
thence to Logres, silently sat her horse.
Now near freedom, she brooded on choice—
this her last errand, but where to cast
her future in seven days' time eluded purpose:
whether with a passport under the King's seal
to return safe to Athens through the themes;
or whether with a dowry to wed some friend;
or to swear herself still of the household, and leave
what end would to come—and then to grieve
perchance for all forgone; the king's poet
lightened no heart except when the heart heightened,
and what heightening was sure to endure such doom?

The gloom of the day hung over the porch;
there the doors swung: the princess Dindrane
came from the house between her two friends,
Elayne and Taliessin, Bors's wife and the king's poet.
Her nature was sweet to all: no call in vain
reached her, but these two she loved—these,
the mistress of a household and the master of verse—held
her heart's world's testimony; her best arts
changed toils with Elayne and studies with Taliessin.
These, her labours and neighbours, brought her that day
to the court of separation, affirmation into rejection.
Vocation before her, Percivale's sister paused,
contemplating the road and the household in waiting.

The slave-girl looked; well she knew the princess,
who in a year and a day had grown dear

to the king's poet's house; she knew the vows
Dindrane rode to take, for the sake of Christ;
she guessed the sword of schism that pierced her lord,
dew-bright as the chrism of dedication
shining already there in Dindrane's brow.
She measured herself against her, in a suddenly now
new-treasured servitude; she saw there
love and a live heart lie in Dindrane
and all circumstance of bondage blessed in her body
moving to a bondage—to a new-panoplied category.
The cell of her own servitude was now the shell
of the body of the princess; therefore, closer, of hers.
The jointed and linked fetters were the jointed bones,
manacles of energy were manipulations of power.
The hazel of the cattle-goad, of the measuring-rod,
of the slaves' discipline, of Logres' highway, of Merlin's
wand of magic, of her lord's line of verse,
of the octave of song, of the footpace under the altar,
straight and strong, was in Dindrane's bare arm,
fair measure in the body of the body's deeds.
Love and a live heart lay in Dindrane;
love and a live heart sprang in the slave,
while the clang of the escort's salute rang in her ears
as she saw moving down the steps the two presences,
Taliessin and Dindrane; rigid were the squires below,
rigid the whole household; at once, in her heart,
servitude and freedom were one and interchangeable.

Servitude is a will that obeys an imaged law;
freedom an unimaged—or makes choice of images.

Dindrane mounted; Taliessin, mounting, said:
'I will ride through the suburbs beside you. Advance, companions.'
His voice lifted the household; they broke to a canter.
As the slave's horse moved beneath her, she saw the lords
riding before her, the Ways upon the Way,
cloaked in the dim day, on the highroad of the hazel
between city and convent, the two great vocations,
the Rejection of all images before the unimaged,
the Affirmation of all images before the all-imaged,
the Rejection affirming, the Affirmation rejecting, the king's poet
riding through a cloud with a vowed novice,
and either no less than the other the doctrine of largesse;
two centaur shapes, cloaked to the haunches;
everywhere centaurs round her on the road, the bush
of hazels everywhere; all rose in the rush
of the company of the household changing to centaur shapes
ranging among the hazels: centaur or hazel
she? slave or free? no centaur; that
for eyes other, if ever—of a child, of a lover,
of the First Mover, of adoration, of a joined future
that should see her new-personal as the king's poet impersonal
had seen her and stated to God—her single future
now her own statement, her statement her function.
The flush of the sap rose within, as without
the rush of the centaurs plunged about her; she grew
to the impersonality of the hazel; before her eyes
the hands of the great personalities linked as they rode,
as they rode fast, close-handed, oath-bonded,
word-in-the-flesh-branded, each seconded
to the other, each in the crowd of Camelot vowed

to the other, the two Ways, the Ways passing
over and through the swelling heart of the hazel,
all the uncut nuts of the hazel ripening to fall
down the cut hazel's way; and it she.

Was there before the King's bailiff a choice?
a voice to return in nostalgia to Athens? to be
free—call it—in Logres? or else to be
compact in an act? to follow the household's heart
in a twin freedom and servitude, an impersonal
time come, the slave made free, the free
bound, Dindrane in a convent, till the whole ended,
ending itself, not she ending it: choice?
no choice then or ever for the king's poet's slave.
She heard in the air, above the centaurs, a voice
drop from the third heaven—fixed is the full.
It was toned to a sweetness of note disowned by the world
while the word was self-owned; as in Merlin's glass
the *mens sensitiva*, the feeling intellect, opens,
and the future comes to pass in a fleeting light,
so, over the galloping household, sang
in the third heaven, overheard above the hooves,
the foster-ward of Dindrane before his birth:
'Fair lord, salute me to my lord Sir Lancelot my father,
and bid him remember of this unstable world.'
The grand Rejection sang to the grand Affirmation;
itself affirming, itself honouring, its peer:
'Salute me, salute me, to my lord Sir Lancelot my father.'

Untie! untie! the two-handed shape

disbanded before her into the two princes.
Taliessin had cried a halt; the air's sound
sang so high it split into his voice,
the voice that followed the art of poetry in Logres,
and another part that fled away singing
into the third heaven; the companions drew rein.
The last villas of Camelot lay behind.
Before her the lords' cloaks shifted as they turned
in their saddles: the king's poet kissed Dindrane's hand.
He said: 'Blessed one, what shall I wish you now
but a safe passage through all the impersonalities?'
And she: 'Most blessed lord, what shall I wish
but the return of the personalities, beyond
the bond and blessing of departure of personality?
I will affirm, my beloved, all that I should.'
And he: 'I will reject all that I should—
yes, and affirm; the term of Camelot, my adored,
lies at the term of Almesbury. The Grace be with you;
which, as your face made visible, let your soul sustain.'
He turned his horse aside; he burned on the household,
crying: 'All, with the princess to Almesbury!
and again to me at Camelot. Dindrane, farewell!'
She cried: 'Taliessin, farewell;' the shell of her body
yearned along the road to the cell of vocation.
Under her hazel's stroke her horse woke
to the gallop; her escort broke to an equal pace;
and her face fixed on the road, only
the other horse the king's poet bestrode
tossed its head in the pause, snorting an answer.

Seven days afterwards, before the king's bailiff,
the slave-girl said: 'I will swear to what I serve,
the household and its future; may God pluck it fair,
for I give my heart to the luck of the hallows: write
that now I am quits with those two jangling bits.
They only can do it with my lord who can do it without him,
and I know he will have about him only those.'

The Founding of the Company

ABOUT this time there grew, throughout Logres,
a new company, as (earlier) in Tabennisi
or (later) on Monte Cassino or in Cappadocia
a few found themselves in common; but this, less—
being purposed only to profess a certain pointing.
It spread first from the household of the king's poet;
it was known by no name, least his own,
who hardly himself knew how it was grown
or whether among the readers or among the grooms
it took source from doctrine or toil, but among his own
it was first nobly spoken as a token of love
between themselves, and between themselves and their lord.
Grounded in the Acts of the Throne and the pacts of the themes,
it lived only by conceded recollection,
having no decision, no vote or admission,
but for the single note that any soul
took of its own election of the Way; the whole
shaped no frame nor titular claim to place.
As the king's name held the high lords
in the kingdom's glory, so the Protection this,
but this was of the commons and the whole manner of love,
when love was fate to minds adult in love.
What says the creed of the Trinity? *quicunque vult;*
therefore its cult was the Trinity and the Flesh-taking,

and its rule as the making of man in the doctrine of largesse,
and its vow as the telling, the singular and mutual confession
of the indwelling, of the mansion and session of each in each.

Grounded so in the Acts and pacts of the Empire,
doctrine and image—from rose-lordly Caucasia
to the sentences sealing the soul through the whole of Logres
by the mouth of London-in-Logres; from the strong base
of maids, porters, mechanics, to the glowing face
of Dindrane (called Blanchfleur) and the cells of the brain
of the king's college and council—were the wise companions.
The king's poet's household opened on the world
in a gay science devised before the world
and prized by (however darkened) the very heathen.
They measured the angle of creation; in three degrees
along the hazel they mounted the mathematics of the soul,
no wisdom separate but for convenience of naming
and the claiming by the intellectual art of its part
in the common union. So, at the first station,
were those who lived by a frankness of honourable exchange,
labour in the kingdom, devotion in the Church, the need
each had of other; this was the measurement and motion
of process—the seed of all civil polity
among Esquimaux or Hottentots, and in any turbulent tribe
the ceasing of strife; only rejected in P'o-l'u,
but only by a nightmare could the household know P'o-l'u.
This the Acts of the Emperor decreed to the world,
losing or loosing none, of the heathen without
or the slaves within; nay, servitude itself
was sweetly fee'd or freed by the willing proffer

of itself to another, the taking of another to itself
in degree, the making of a mutual beauty in exchange,
be the exchange dutiful or freely debonair;
duty so and debonair freedom mingled,
taking and giving being the living of largesse,
and in less than this the kingdom having no saving.

The Company's second mode bore farther
the labour and fruition; it exchanged the proper self
and wherever need was drew breath daily
in another's place, according to the grace of the Spirit
'dying each other's life, living each other's death'.
Terrible and lovely is the general substitution of souls
the Flesh-taking ordained for its mortal images
in its first creation, and now in Its sublime self
shows, since It deigned to be dead in the stead of each man.
This to be practised the hidden contemplatives knew
throughout the Empire, and daily slew and were slain;
this to be practised the whole Company believed
and gently and sweetly received in the shining air
even at Camelot; at Caerleon it became common—
there when they removed they loved easier.
This now out of the cells of contemplatives
walked for a little in the sun; none of the Company—
in marriage, in the priesthood, in friendship, in all love—
forgot in their own degree the decree of substitution.
Wary of much chatter, yet when they kissed
or pressed hands, they claimed and were claimed at once,
neither ashamed of taking nor chary of giving,
love becoming fate to dedicate souls.

Few—and that hardly—entered on the third
station, where the full salvation of all souls
is seen, and their co-inhering, as when the Trinity
first made man in Their image, and now restored
by the one adored substitution; there men
were known, each alone and none alone,
bearing and borne, as the Flesh-taking sufficed
the God-bearer to make her a sharer in Itself.
Of the lords—Percivale, Dindrane, Dinadan, the Archbishop;
of the people—a mechanic here, a maid there,
knew the whole charge, as vocation devised.
More rarely, at a moment, the king's poet saw
in the large vision of verse, at once everywhere
the law willed and fulfilled and walking in Camelot;
as from a high deck among tossing seas
beyond Broceliande he had seen afar
a deep, strange island of granite growth,
thrice charged with massive light in change,
clear and golden-cream and rose tinctured,
each in turn the Holder and the Held—as the eyes
of the watcher altered and faltered and again saw
the primal Nature revealed as a law to the creature;
beyond Carbonek, beyond Broceliande,
in the land of the Trinity, the land of the perichoresis,
of separateness without separation, reality without rift,
where the Basis is in the Image, and the Image in the Gift,
the Gift is in the Image and the Image in the Basis,
and Basis and Gift alike in Gift and Basis.

On a Sunday, on a feast of All Fools, Dinadan came

to the rose-garden where Taliessin walked.
The king's poet ached with belated verse;
he took part against himself; his heart waited
for his voice, and again his voice for his dumb heart.
He dreamed of the face of Dindrane; the face of Dinadan
suddenly before him was compact of trifold light,
as by an analogical substitution
for Dindrane or the vision of verse—truth from the taunt,
and the proof, for those who will, of the vaunt of the doctrine.
Dinadan said: 'Well encountered, lieutenant
(they call you) of God's new grace in the streets of Camelot.'
Taliessin answered: 'What should I do, calling
myself a master, and falling so to P'o-l'u?
I should rue the boast there among the marshes,
a lieutenant of the octopods for ever.' Dinadan said:
'Sir, God is the origin and the end God;
cause is comfort and high comfort is cause.
Catch as catch can—but the higher caught in the lower,
the lower in the higher; any buyer of souls
is bought himself by his purchase; take the lieutenancy
for the sake of the shyness the excellent absurdity holds.'
Taliessin said: 'Must I be once more superfluous?
as to Dindrane and the kingdom, so to the Company,
verse is superfluous, and I even to verse.'
Dinadan answered: 'Sir, in the charge at Badon
and the taking of Camelot, though you were chief, you were still
superfluous; could relief ever have come with forsaking
the masculine hearts of your house, who on each side
cried as they rode: "Taliessin! and charge, Logres!"'?
Labour without grudge is without grief,

and the dayspring will have its head where it bids.
Any may be; one must. To neighbour
whom and as the Omnipotence wills is a fetch
of grace; the lowest wretch is called greatest
—and may be—on the feast of fools. The God-bearer
is the prime and sublime image of entire superfluity.
If an image lacks, since God backs all,
be the image, a needless image of peace
to those in peace; to you an image of modesty.
This purchase of modesty is nothing new;
in the cause is your comfort, in your comfort also the cause.
Take the largesse; think yourself the less; bless heaven.'

Therefore in Camelot and Caerleon the king's poet
was rated then, by the unformulated Company,
as, beyond the principle and the rule, their single bond.
Unvowed, they allowed the lieutenancy in Camelot, but on feasts
served it in Caerleon with such a delicate smile,
such joyous and high-restrained obeisance of laughter
as (more than in all households of the great lords)
ordained through all degrees an equality of being.
The Company throve by love, by increase of peace,
by the shyness of saving and being saved in others—
the Christ-taunting and Christ-planting maxim
which throughout Logres the excellent absurdity held.

The Queen's Servant

THE lord Kay wrote to the lord Taliessin:
'Now the queen's majesty has need of a maid
for certain works—to read Greek and translate,
to manage the building of rose-gardens, to wait
about her in actions of office; one who knows
the rhythms of ceremony, also of the grand art.
The house of Your Sublimity, besides its name in battle,
sends forth a fame of such knowledgeable creatures; please
the king's poet to sign this warrant I send,
adding what name he choose to bear it back.'

Taliessin sent for one of his proved household,
proper to the summons, near his thought. She came;
he exhibited the warrant, saying: 'Now be free.
The royalties of Logres are not slavishly served,
nor have you deserved these years less of Us
than to go to the queen's meinie.' She said: 'So.
Freedom, I see, is the final task of servitude.
Yet buy, sir, still what was bought in your thought—
myself with a clear sum purchased from the world.
Though I pay the ransom now, it is but with your gold;
hold well now to the purpose of the purchase.
How shall I serve else?' He said: 'The spells
of Merlin were mighty in time, but rhyme trebles

the significance of time. Where once did We buy you?'
She answered: 'In a shire of Caucasia, when my lord,
growing in glory of song, passed from Byzantium
eastward through Caucasia.' He said: 'The lambs
that wander among roses of Caucasia are golden-lamped.
I have seen from its blue skies a flurry of snow
bright as a sudden irrepressible smile
drive across a golden-fleeced landscape.'
'Nay,' she said, 'though I was bought there,
have I ever seen such a place? Sir, what shire
is noted for such fair weather?' He answered: 'Read
the maps in Merlin's books or Ours or the one
small title We brought by the Emperor's leave from Byzantium.
Or even learn it a quicker way. Unclothe.
We who bought you furnish you. As was Our thought,
so be the truth, for Our thought was as the truth.
Know by Our sight the Rite that invokes Sarras
lively and lifelong. O We most unworthy!'
She cast her garments from her; shining-naked
and rose-flushed she stood; in that calm air,
fair body and fair soul one organic
whole—so the purchase, so the purpose,
the prayer of Dindrane in the convent at Almesbury so
and the benediction (unspoken yet) of Galahad
on all the derivations. The lord Taliessin
said: 'And so, in a high eirenical shire,
are flashing flaunts of snow across azure skies,
golden fleeces, and gardens of deep roses.
There, through the rondures, eyes as quick as clear
see, small but very certain, Byzantium,

or even in a hope the beyond-sea meadows
that, as in a trope of verse, Caucasia shadows.
Uncurtain the roses.' He named a blessing from Merlin,
and she stretched her open hands to the air; there
they were full at once of roses; again and again
she gathered and flung them at Taliessin's feet—
brushing off buds that clung to her, crimson, centifoliae,
Caucasian roses gently falling in Camelot.
Art-magic spiritual, they neither faded
nor vanished; so holy, over all wizards, was Merlin.
The whole room was shaded crimson from them.
Taliessin lifted his hand; she stayed; he sang
a sweet borrowed craft from Broceliande,
and the room grew full at once of the bleat of lambs.
Visibly forming, there fell on the heaped roses
tangles and curds of golden wool; the air
was moted gold in the rose-tinctured chamber—
as in the land of the Trinity those few
who have seen say that the light is clear or roseal
or golden-cream, each in each and again in each.
Taliessin said: 'Thus the gathering through Broceliande
of the riches of Caucasia; but We—did We not see
a poet in Italy do more for a beggar
by the grace of our Lord? neither wizard nor saint
are We, yet something perhaps—Let the Flesh-taking
aid Us now for the making of Your Excellency's coat,
if it please the Mercy.' Thrice he genuflected,
thrice he murmured inaudible Latin, thrice
with blessed hands he touched the roses and the wool.
The roses climbed round her; shoulder to knee,

they clung and twined and changed to a crimson kirtle.
The wool rose gently on no wind,
and was flung to her shoulders; behind her, woven of itself,
it fell in full folds to a gold-creamed cloak;
hued almost as the soft redeemed flesh
hiding the flush of the rich redeemed blood
in the land of the Trinity, where the Holy Ghost works
creation and sanctification of flesh and blood.
Taliessin fastened the cloak with his own brooch
at her throat; only he drew round her the old
leathern girdle, for a bond and a quiet oath
to gather freedom as once she gathered servitude.
Shoes he fetched her from the household's best store,
to wear still the recollection of her peers,
under whatever election she graced them still.
Clothed and brilliant, she faced the king's poet.
He said: 'So bright? yet be seen now in Camelot.'
The colour's height about her a little quenched
its power; she, still drenched by the power,
murmured: 'Let my lord end this hour with a gift
other than the Rite; that the Rite be certain, let
my lord seal me to it and it to me.'
Gravely, considering the work, the king's poet said:
'As the Roman master sets his bondman free?
or the bishop in the Roman rite the instructed neophyte
at his proper confirmation?' She said: 'To choose
were insolence too much and of too strange a kind;
my lord knows my mind.' Her eyes were set
upon him, companion to companion, peer to peer.
He sent his energy wholly into hers.

'Nay,' he said, 'henceforth, in the queen's house,
be but the nothing We made you, making you something.'
Lightly he struck her face; at once the blast
of union struck her heart, the art-magic
blended fast with herself, while all she
burned before him, colour of cloak and kirtle
surpassed by colour of flesh and blood and soul
whole and organic in the divined redemption
after the kind of Christ and the order of Logres.
He said: 'Till death and after,' and she: 'Till death,
and so long as the whole creation has any being,
the derivation is certain, and the doom accomplished.'

In his room at Camelot the king's poet signed
the warrant; he gave it to the queen's free servant,
saying: 'Carry this to the lord Kay, companion.
Be as Ourself in Logres; be as Dindrane
under the Protection, and in the Protection prosper.
Depart, with God.' She said: 'Remain, in God.'

The Meditation of Mordred

THE king has poled his horsemen across the Channel
on the torn fragments of letters from the Pope Deodatus:
setting private affairs in front of public,
he has left to me the power of the kingdom and the glory.

He has dragged up all his elms; they were the poles.
Now they stand immobilized round Lancelot in Benwick;
lest, having one illegal son by his sister my mother,
the king should be cheated with another by his wife the queen

He ravages Gaul; I rest on his palace roof,
and watch the elms bud in steel points
with which Gawaine and my uncanonical father
prod Lancelot's walls; Lancelot sits safe.

The queen hides at Almesbury among the nuns.
If I pulled her out and paraded her through Camelot,
the town would laugh and howl in a mania of righteousness,
casting missiles visible and invisible, words and stones.

Camelot is apt to maintain a double poise
of Catholic morals and another kind of catholic mockery.
It is laidly alike to be a wittol and a whore,
and wittoldom and whoredom are alike good cause for war.

The elms top the Gallic sky; the Pope
bade Arthur be friends again with his friend, but the king
tore the pontifical letters; would not the Pope
(the thing done) be pleased if his seal were avenged?

London is become a forest; voices and arms
throw a dementia of hands, tossed caps,
towzled shouts, bare grinning leaves,
a whole wood of moral wantons, whose spines

are tree-stretched up towards me, their hope.
Arthur had his importance; why not I?
Like son, like father; *adsum,*
said the steel trap to the wolf when the trap sprang.

The nit-witted wittols or wordly wisdom tear
their throats at the abolition of the Byzantine tribute,
now the coined dragons stay in their pockets at home.
Kin to kin presently, children; I too am a dragon.

My father dwelled on the thought of the Grail for his luck,
but I can manage without such fairy mechanism.
If it does prove to be, which is no likely thought,
I will send my own dozen of knights to pull it in.

My cooks would be glad of such a cauldron of Ceridwen
to stand by their fires—magic; but, come to magic,
at a rubbing genii might slide into my room,
delicately, as in the kitchen of Ala-ud-Din.

Ala-ud-Din . . . he dwelled beyond miles of bamboo,
of bamboo moving with waving tops in the wind,
beyond the isles and the lands whose names I heard
from Zemarchus the trader who travelled the turn of the seas;

by water beyond the islands of Naked Men
and the province of the Five Senses; beyond P'o-l'u
he told of another Empire, beyond the bamboos,
where a small Emperor sits, whom his women fan

in the green palace among his yellow seas.
He watches his tiny-footed, slant-eyed wives
creep in and out; he deigns
a rare caress to any he cares to praise.

Once or twice in each seven years
he relieves himself by softly breathing a name;
if with the music, they bear her to his silken bed;
if against, they carry her in a coffer of bamboo bars

to lie on the edge of a swamp till thirst or the flood
or the crocodiles end her, but the coolies slink away
from her caged there, and crawl with prostrations
back under the curved eaves of the palace of jade.

Here, as he in the antipodean seas,
I will have my choice, and be adored for the having;
when my father King Arthur has fallen in the wood of his elms,
I will sit here aione in a kingdom of Paradise.

The Prayers of the Pope

EARLY on the feast of Christmas the young Pope
knelt in Lateran—Deodatus, Egyptian-born,
slender, white-haired, incandescent,
seeming in his trance of prayer a third twin
of Merlin and Brisen, masculine touched with the feminine,
except for their black hair strangely bleached
as if time's metre were smitten by sacred grief.
Over the altar a reliquary of glass held
an intinctured Body; the Pope waited to pass
to sing his tri-fold Eucharist; meanwhile he prayed
alone and aloud in the candled shroud of the dark.
Sweet his voice sounded in the new Latin
founded on Virgil but colloquial, capable of rhyme,
fastening in a time of genesis Lupercal and Lateran
and hastening by measure the flood of the soul in the blood.
The young Pontiff's meditation set to *Magnificat*,·
to the total Birth intending the total Death,
to the Love that lost Itself, nor only an image
nor only all the images but wholly Itself.
The Pope prayed: 'But each loss of each image
is single and full, a thing unrequited,
plighted in presence to no recompense, no
purchase of paradise; eyes see no future:

when the Son of Man comes, he brings no faith in a future.
Send not, send not, the rich empty away.'

A tale that emerged from Logres surged in Europe
and swelled in the Pope's ears; it held nothing
of fulfilment of prophecy and the sea-coming of the Grail
but only of bleak wars between Arthur and Lancelot,
Gawaine set to seek his heart's vengeance,
the king's son gone whoring with fantasy,
and mobs roaring through Camelot; the Pope's letters
had brought no staying of the slaying nor ceasing of the sin
nor healed the dichotomy of battle. The tale spread,
till the governors of the themes knew it in their own dreams;
forsaking the Emperor, they chose among themselves,
here one and there one, foes
among themselves, puppets of reputation,
void of communicated generation of glory;
clouds covered the Imperial Throne in Byzantium;
and the Acts of the Throne were let by infidels; none
cared how men were shaped in body or mind,
nor pined for the perfect Parousia; all gave
their choice to the primal curse and the grave; their loves
escaped back to the old necromantic gnosis
of separation, were it but from one soul.
Frantic with fear of losing themselves in others,
they denounced and delivered one other to reprobation—
Mordred or the Khan of the Huns or the Khalif of Asia
or any neighbour they envied in labour or love.
They rejected the City; they made substitutes for the City;
mutes or rhetoricians instead of the sacred poets,

cheating for charity, exposition for experience,
braggadocio or burlesque for faith and hope.

The Pope prayed before the Body in Lateran:
'Rich in sorrow, rich in heart's heaviness,
blessed are we, bearing soul's wealth now,
and cannot anyhow part with that wealth, laden
with loss, and the loss always an affirmation,
double affirmation—image and the opposite of image—
which our wit, as courteously thine, O Blessed, carries,
but thine thyself only and the lack of thyself;
send not, send not, the rich empty away.'

The line faltered along the Danube and the Rhine;
pale in London and Lutetia grew the tale of peace,
and bloody the Noel-song; the towns of Logres
felt the sliding planes of the raiders' sails,
and Gaul all the push of the Northern woods,
savage growths, moods infinitely multiplied
across the bleak plains, under rains and snows
of myths bitter to bondage, where in race
by sullen marshes separated from race
virtue is monopolized and grace prized in schism.
The consuls and lords fought for the fords and towns,
but over the Rhine, over the Vistula and Danube
pressed the grand tribes; the land shook
as band after band stamped into darkness cities
whose burning had lamped their path; their wrath grew
with vengeance and victory; they looked to no returning.

The Pope prayed: 'Where is difference between us?
What does the line along the rivers define?
Causes and catapults they have and we have,
and the death of a brave beauty is mutual everywhere
If there be difference, it must be in thy sense
that we declare—O Blessed, pardon affirmation!—
and they deny—O Blessed, pardon negation!—
that we derive from them and they from us,
and alive are they in us and we in them.
We know how we have sinned; we know not how they.
Intend for us the double wealth of repentance;
send not, send not, the rich empty away.'

Now within the frontiers, the evil wizards,
the seers of the heathen, with thumbs instead of fingers,
marked on the earth the reversed and accursed pentagram;
they lit and fed the flickering spectral flames
of the rituals of necromancy; they poured on the fires
mastic and gum-aromatic; they uttered invocation
of smouldering deities whose very names were lost,
but the half-broken and half-spoken syllables
wrought resurrection in the Pit; yet even those wizards
hid their eyes where some few, their chief,
the beastliest and chillest in blasphemy, called farther
on the powers of P'o-l'u, on the antipodean octopods,
on the slime that had been before the time of Merlin
and below the trees and seas of Broceliande.
Then, in that power, they called and enthralled the dead,
the poor, long-dead, long-buried, decomposing
shapes of humanity; the earthy shapes stirred,

all whom the governors of the themes had once slain,
the uneyed images of old blockade and barricade,
children starved in sieges, prostituted women,
men made slaves or crucified; before the Parousia,
before the Redemption made manifest, the poor bodies
were drawn again slowly up through the earth,
and, held steady on their feet, stood and answered.
With rods of desecrated hazel the sorcerers
touched them and bade them walk; bloodless, automatized,
precursors of the tribes in a necromancy of justice,
those mechanized bodies stalked across the fords,
and the hordes of the heathen followed the corpses to battle.
Consuls and lords felt the cold coming
and the drumming of the earth under the tribes, but they shrank
only before the ghosts of the past—from graves
drawn by maleficent spells, but too-veritable ghosts
before those hosts moving in a terrible twilight.

The Pope saw himself—he sighed and prayed—
as a ruin of the Empire; he died in a foreboding.
He felt within him the themes divide, each
dreadfully autonomous in its own corporal place,
its virtue monopolized, its grace prized, in schism,
and the little insane brain whimpering of pain
and its past; before the Parousia, before the Redemption,
all his unredeemed deeds and words
rose as once they had been, fire in his body,
chill in his mind, and everywhere in mind and body
the terrible schism of identity into the categories
and the miserable conquest of the categories over identity

split all, and fatally separated the themes
which in the beginning were mated with identical glory.
Such is death's outrage; so the Pope
died in a foretasting; only, hasting
still to the salvaged and re-engaged Body,
he prayed: 'And for me, in that new day, O Blessed,
send not, send not, the rich empty away.'

Against the rule of the Emperor the indivisible
Empire was divided; therefore the Parousia suspended
its coming, and abode still in the land of the Trinity.
Logres was void of Grail and Crown, but well
had Mordred spelled his lesson from his father King Arthur.
The prince had hungered; he had waited to-morrow and to-
    morrow
till the sorrow of his waiting, satiating his blood,
drove him to change the double wealth of loss
for the single having; his craving refused itself.
He sought his vision by mere derision of the vision.
He drew into the ordained place of the Table
the unstable pagan chiefs; all personal
griefs in Logres burst and curst the impersonal
formulae of glory; he assuaged his own image
with the image of the Throne, setting both against the Empire,
and begetting by the succubus of his longing, in a world
    of pagans,
the falsity of all images and their incoherence.

The Pope prayed: 'O Blessed, confirm
nor thee in thine images only but thine images in thee.

Bestow now the double inseparable wonder,
the irrevocable union: set in each thy term.
The formulae of glory are the food of intellectual love,
from the rose-gardens to the wardens of the divine science,
and so to the sacred Heart; the Flesh-taker
with the God-bearer, each the off-springing of other,
the Maker a sharer only and the making as much.
Let the chief of the images touch the Unimaged, and free
the Love that recovered Itself, nor only an image,
nor only all the images, but wholly Itself;
free It that we, solely the rich, may pray
send not, send not, the rich empty away.'

Taliessin gathered his people before the battle.
'Peers of the household,' the king's poet said,
'dead now, save Lancelot, are the great lords
and the Table may end to-morrow; if it live,
it shall have new names in a new report.
Short is Our time, though that time prove eternal.
Therefore'—he lifted his hands to the level of his brow,
the hands that had written and harped the king's music;
there the ageing began ere the hair was grey,
or the tongue tired of song, or the brain fey;
O but the Bright Forehead was once young!
'Therefore now We dissolve the former bonds—'
the voice sounded, the hands descended—'We dissolve
the outer bonds; We declare the Company still
fixed in the will of all who serve the Company,
but the ends are on Us, peers and friends; We restore
again to God the once-permitted lieutenancy;

blessed be Dinadan by whom the lieutenancy began
when he called Us on the day of fools, on his own day.
We restore it to God in each singly and in all.
Receive it in God.' One of the household said,
shining through grief, the king's poet's steward,
a strong star: 'This is the last largesse;
give we freely, companions; but first, lord,
let us live again the moment of ratification,
a superfluous necessity; let us lay our hands again
between my lord's, and swear that the household endures
for ever, and we yours in it.' Taliessin
answered: 'What skill have We had but to be the will
of the whole Company?—We a needful superfluity,
the air in which the summer stars shine,
nay, less—the mode only of their placing and gracing.
It is a command; swear.' While it was done,
lightly each in turn and each with the other,
and each with the king's poet, the least of his household,
all the household exchanged the kiss of peace.

The Pope prayed: 'Keep thy own for thyself.
When the Thrones vanish—the imperial Throne hidden,
the vassal thrones changed—and forbidden lives
floating about the headless Emperor in P'o-l'u—
keep thy word in thine unknown elect:
no wise their supernatural parts sundered
from their natural hearts; little shall those hearts suffer—
so much shall the healing metaphysic have power upon them—
from evil and mischief and the crafty assaults of the devil.
Purely their souls shall go and their bodies securely,

whether in body or soul they drink deadly,
or handle malice and slander as they handle serpents,
by the magnificence in modesty, the modesty in magnificence
that the doctrine of largesse teaches; what recovers
lovers in lovers is love; let them then
go into every den of magic and mutiny,
touch the sick and the sick be healed, take
the trick of the weak devils with peace, and speak
at last on the coast of the land of the Trinity the tongue
of the Holy Ghost. O Blessed, for ever bring
thine own to thyself and for ever thyself to thine own.'

Jupiter rode over Carbonek; beyond Jupiter,
beyond the summer stars, deep heaven
centrally opened within the land of the Trinity;
planetary light was absorbed there, and emerged
again in its blissful journeys; there the three
lords of the quest landed from the vessel of the quest,
Bors, Percivale, and Galahad the High Prince—
the chief of the images, and the contemplation of the images,
and the work of the images in all degrees of the world.
They lay for a year and a day imprisoned in a trance,
waiting among moving rocks and granite voices
the dawn-hour of the trine-toned light
and they in fine drawn to the canon of the Grail.
Whereof afterwards Bors should bear to Logres
the tale in his heart and the last largesse of Galahad.
He should follow the sun; which now behind the lords
rose from the saffron veil that, on the deck,
covered the body of Dindrane, Percivale's sister,

Taliessin's love, Galahad's foster-warden.
The sun outward ran a year s journey;
the earth span around the sun for a year;
for a year and a day the lords lay entranced.
The sun ran; it saw, and shuddered as it ran,
the bounds of the Empire breaking; beyond P'o-l'u
it saw the giant octopods moving; their tentacles
waving, stretching, stealing souls from the shores,
feeling along Burma, nearing India,
appearing above ocean, or sinking and slinking
and spreading everywhere along the bottom of ocean,
and heading inward. But there they touched and clutched,
somewhere in the deep seas, something that invited
holding—and they held, enfolding—and the tentacles folded
round long, stretched limbs, like somewhat of themselves
but harder and huger; the tentacles were touched and clutched,
flung and were clung to, clung and were not flung off,
brainlessly hastened and brainfully were hastened to.
The roots of Broceliande fastened on them
length lying along length and gripping length;
in the ocean where near and far are infinite and equal
the hollow suckers of the vast slimy tentacles
were tautened to Nimue's trees through the seas of P'o-l'u,
and fixed to a regimen; held so for ever
to know for ever nothing but their own hypnotic
sucking at the harsh roots; the giant octopods
hung helpless; the wizards and gods of the heathen
far along the Northern line, beyond Rhine and Danube,
helpless dwindled; helpless, the headless Emperor
was loosened, and sank and dissolved in the uncoped seas,

a crimson tincture, a formless colour, the foul
image of the rose-gardens of Caucasia now
losing itself, drifting in the waters, and none
to know what was real and what unreal
or what of sense stayed in the vagrant phosphorescence
save the deep impassable Trinity in the land of the Trinity,
uttering unsearchable bliss. The lords stirred
as the triple-toned light broke upon them
and they heard in their mode the primal canon of the Grail.
The roses of the world bloomed from Burma to Logres;
pure and secure from the lost tentacles of P'o-l'u,
the women of Burma walked with the women of Caerleon.

The Pope prayed: 'Thou hast harried hell, O Blessed,
and carried thence the least token of thyself.
Thou hast spoken a word of power in the midst of hell,
and well are thine Acts everywhere qualified with eternity.
That Thou only canst be, Thou only
everywhere art; let hell also confess thee,
bless thee, praise thee, and magnify thee for ever.'

The Pope passed to sing the Christmas Eucharist.
He invoked peace on the bodies and souls of the dead,
yoked fast to him and he to them,
co-inherent all in Adam and all in Christ.
The magical march of the dead by Rhine and Danube
and the tread of the necromancers who affirm only
vengeance and value of victory he lonely
received; he sheaved there the corn of his prayer.
The gnosis of separation in the Pope's soul

had become a promulgation of sacred union,
and he his function only; at the junction of communion
he offered his soul's health for the living corpses,
his guilt, his richness of repentance, wealth for woe.
This was the Pope's prayer; prayer is substance;
quick the crowd, the thick souls of the dead,
moved in the Pope's substance to the invoked Body,
the Body of the Eucharist, the Body of the total loss,
the unimaged loss; the Body salvaged the bodies
in the fair, sweet strength of the Pope's prayer.
The easement of exchange led into Christ's appeasement
under the heart-breaking manual acts of the Pope.
Before the host on the rivers, the automatized corpses
stopped, dropped, disintegrated to dust;
and the lust of the evil magicians hung in the air
helpless; consuls and lords within the Empire,
for all the darkening of the Empire and the loss of Logres
and the hiding of the High Prince, felt the Empire
revive in a live hope of the Sacred City.

Kneeling after the Eucharist, the Pope said,
for the riches of loss, *Magnificat;* prostrate, he prayed:
'Send not, send not, the rich empty away.'

CPSIA information can be obtained
at www.ICGtesting.com
Printed in the USA
BVOW09s0836310517
485616BV00003B/162/P